THE 4th (QUEEN'S OWN) HUSSARS
IN THE GREAT WAR

OFFICERS, 4TH (QUEEN'S OWN) HUSSARS, CURRAGH, JUNE, 1914.

Photo by] [Gale & Polden, Ltd.

Capt. T. W. Pragnell Lt. K. C. North 2/Lt. M. F. Radclyffe Lt. R. J. V. Falkner 2/Lt. G. G. F. Greville Lt. J. D. Pibby 2/Lt. J. R. Lonsdale Lt. H. K. D. Evans 2/Lt. B. B. Falkner Capt. B. Blood
(Killed) (Wounded twice) (Killed) (Wounded & Prisoner) (Killed) (Wounded & Prisoner) (Killed)

Maj. H. B. Mockett Maj. P. Howell Lt.-Col. I. G. Hogg, D.S.O. Maj. J. E. C. Darley Capt. & Adjt. A. V. W. Stokes
(Wounded) (Killed) (Killed) (Killed) (Wounded)

2/Lt. C. C. Henry 2/Lt. J. H. Sword Lt. & Q.-M. G. R. Burton 2/Lt. G. A. Heinekey Lt. W. A. C. Heyman
(Killed) (Killed)

THE
4th (QUEEN'S OWN) HUSSARS IN THE GREAT WAR

BY
CAPTAIN H. K. D. EVANS, M.C.
AND CHAPTERS IX AND X BY
MAJOR N. O. LAING, D.S.O

WITH A FOREWORD BY
RIGHT HON. WINSTON CHURCHILL, P.C.

Dedicated
TO
THE 4th (QUEEN'S OWN) HUSSARS
PAST, PRESENT AND FUTURE

FOREWORD

THIS plain yet careful record of the fortunes and services of the 4th (Queen's Own) Hussars in the Great War deserves and will repay attentive study from those to whom the history of the regiments of the British Army is of vivid interest. The records of the 4th Light Dragoons in the Peninsula and Crimea were very scantily kept, and much that would have been of real instruction and inspiration to other generations of officers and men has passed altogether out of human reach. In these pages we may follow step by step in full detail the movements of a cavalry regiment through the whole of the five campaigns in France. The vitally important cavalry work of the Retreat from Mons was succeeded by a prolonged period when the trenches stretched from the sea to the Alps, when there were no flanks for cavalry to turn and no war of movement for their manœuvring capacity. As the British Army grew, division by division, from the small original Expeditionary Force to a total strength of about two million men, no proportionate increase was made in the cavalry. On the contrary, it became actually smaller, and a single cavalry corps sufficed in the last phase of the war for all the requirements of a British Army of nearly sixty divisions. This unique body of horsemen, with their power of intensely rapid movement across country, became the one mobile reserve on which Lord French and Lord Haig in turn counted to throw into any gap that might be made in the front by the sudden attack of the enemy. As such, the cavalry rendered services of the utmost importance in each successive year of the war. In addition, they took their turn in the trenches whenever it was possible to spare them from their paramount duty.

It is true that the fond hopes which cavalry Generals and cavalry soldiers cherished of a great irruption of cavalry through the German lines as the culmination of a decisive battle never materialized; and surely we may now say that they never could have materialized against an enemy so strongly posted and entrenched and so well organized as the Germans. But, although this supreme success did not fall to the British cavalry in France, the part they played in maintaining the front and securing the final victory will be increasingly appreciated and understood as the after-study of the Great War progresses. And in that task the 4th Hussars played, as will be seen from these pages, an honourable and distinguished part, sustaining and in many respects surpassing the finest deeds in their annals of the past.

WINSTON S. CHURCHILL.

August 31st, 1920.

APPENDICES

APPENDIX A

PAGE

ACTION OF 2ND CAVALRY DIVISION (WITH CANADIAN CAVALRY DIVISION ATTACHED) IN FRONT OF AMIENS, 30TH MARCH–1ST APRIL, 1918 141

APPENDIX B

2ND CAVALRY DIVISION: NARRATIVE OF OPERATIONS, 1ST APRIL, 1918 147

APPENDIX C

SUMMARY OF OPERATIONS FROM 18TH OCTOBER TO 11TH NOVEMBER, 1918 150

APPENDIX D

LETTERS OF APPRECIATION 160

APPENDIX E

REPORT ON WIELTJE, 2ND MAY, 1915 162

APPENDIX F

HONOURS AND AWARDS 165

APPENDIX G

OFFICERS PRESENT WITH THE REGIMENT AT 11 A.M., 11TH NOVEMBER 1918 173

APPENDIX H

	PAGE
Nominal Roll of Officers Embarking at Dublin, 15th August, 1914	174

APPENDIX I

Roll of Officers, Warrant Officers, Non-Commissioned Officers and Men who Served continuously with the Regiment between 14th August, 1914, and 11th November, 1918 ... 175

APPENDIX J

Roll of Warrant and Non-Commissioned Officers and Men Serving with the Regiment who obtained Commissions during the War ... 177

APPENDIX K

Nominal Roll of Officers who Died during the War, 4th August, 1914 to 11th November, 1918	179
Nominal Roll of Men who Died during the War, 4th August, 1914 to 11th November 1918	180
Nominal Roll of Officers Wounded during the War, 4th August, 1914 to 11th November, 1918	183
Nominal Roll of Men Wounded during the War, 4th August, 1914 to 11th November, 1918	184

CONTENTS

CHAPTER I

MOBILIZATION—ARRIVAL IN FRANCE—THE RETREAT FROM MONS ... 1

CHAPTER II

THE ADVANCE TO THE AISNE—BILLETS IN BRAINE ... 13

CHAPTER III

FROM THE AISNE TO THE FIRST BATTLE OF YPRES ... 22

CHAPTER IV

20TH OCTOBER–20TH NOVEMBER, 1914 : FIRST BATTLE OF YPRES—HOLLEBEKE—WULVERGHEM—HERENTHAGE CHATEAU ... 31

CHAPTER V

21ST NOVEMBER, 1914–22ND APRIL, 1915 : WINTER QUARTERS, 1914–15—ZILLEBEKE TRENCHES—LIEUT.-COLONEL RANKIN TAKES OVER COMMAND ... 49

CHAPTER VI

23RD APRIL–30TH MAY, 1915 : FIRST GERMAN GAS ATTACK—WIELTJE—HOOGE ... 59

CHAPTER VII

31ST MAY, 1915–15TH MARCH, 1917 : THE SUMMER OF 1915—BATTLE OF LOOS—WINTER QUARTERS, 1915–16—VERMELLES TRENCHES—SOMME BATTLE, 1916—WINTER QUARTERS, 1916–17 69

CHAPTER VIII

5TH APRIL, 1917–20TH MARCH, 1918 : BATTLE OF ARRAS TO THE BEGINNING OF THE GERMAN OFFENSIVE IN MARCH, 1918 ... 79

CHAPTER IX

21ST MARCH–22ND JULY, 1918 : THE GREAT GERMAN OFFENSIVE   96

CHAPTER X

23RD JULY–11TH NOVEMBER, 1918 : THE VICTORY OFFENSIVE   118

ILLUSTRATIONS

OFFICERS, 4TH HUSSARS, JUNE, 1914 ... ... *Frontispiece*	
	Facing page
1. REGIMENT ON BOARD S.S. "ATLANTIAN," SAILING FROM DUBLIN, AUGUST 15TH, 1914.—2 AND 3. EMBARKING AT DUBLIN, AUGUST 15TH, 1914	17
1. CPL. WAKEFIELD, 4TH HUSSARS, WITH GERMAN PRISONER, SEPTEMBER, 1914.—2. WATERING IN THE RIVER MARNE NEAR MEAUX, SEPTEMBER 4TH, 1914.—3. "A" SQUADRON NEAR FRIERS, AUGUST 28TH, 1914; THE LATE LIEUT.-COL. J. E. DARLEY IN FOREGROUND.—4. REGIMENT OFF-SADDLED NEAR NOUVRON, AUGUST 30TH, 1914.—5. 2ND TROOP "A" SQUADRON, CHAUNY, AUGUST 29TH, 1914.—6. ON THE MARCH, DECEMBER, 1914	48
BRIGADIER-GENERAL C. RANKIN, C.M.G., D.S.O., WHO COMMANDED THE 4TH HUSSARS FROM MARCH, 1915, TO APRIL 16TH, 1916	76
1. A CORNER OF YPRES, 1915.—2. 1ST TROOP, "A" SQUADRON, RESTING ON CANAL NORTH OF YPRES THE DAY AFTER THE FIRST GERMAN GAS ATTACK.—3. "A" SQUADRON NEAR WARGNIES LE GRAND, AUGUST 29TH, 1914.—4. "A" SQUADRON AT ELOUGES, AUGUST 23RD, 1914	87
MAJOR (TEMP. LIEUT.-COLONEL) N. O. LAING, D.S.O. ...	110
1. RETURNING FROM TRENCHES NEAR HOLLEBEKE, OCTOBER, 1914.—2. CHURCH PARADE, LE PARC, MARCH, 1915.—3. POTIJZE, MAY 14TH, 1915.—4. SQUADRON BATHS, DECEMBER, 1914	144

MAPS

Battle of 24th August, 1914

Western Theatre of War

Country Round Ypres

The Fighting Round Hollebeke, October, 1914

Trenches at Vermelles, January, 1916

The Fighting Round Moreuil, March, 1918

30th March—1st April, 1918

THE MAPS IN THIS REPRINT
ARE PLACED AFTER THIS PAGE

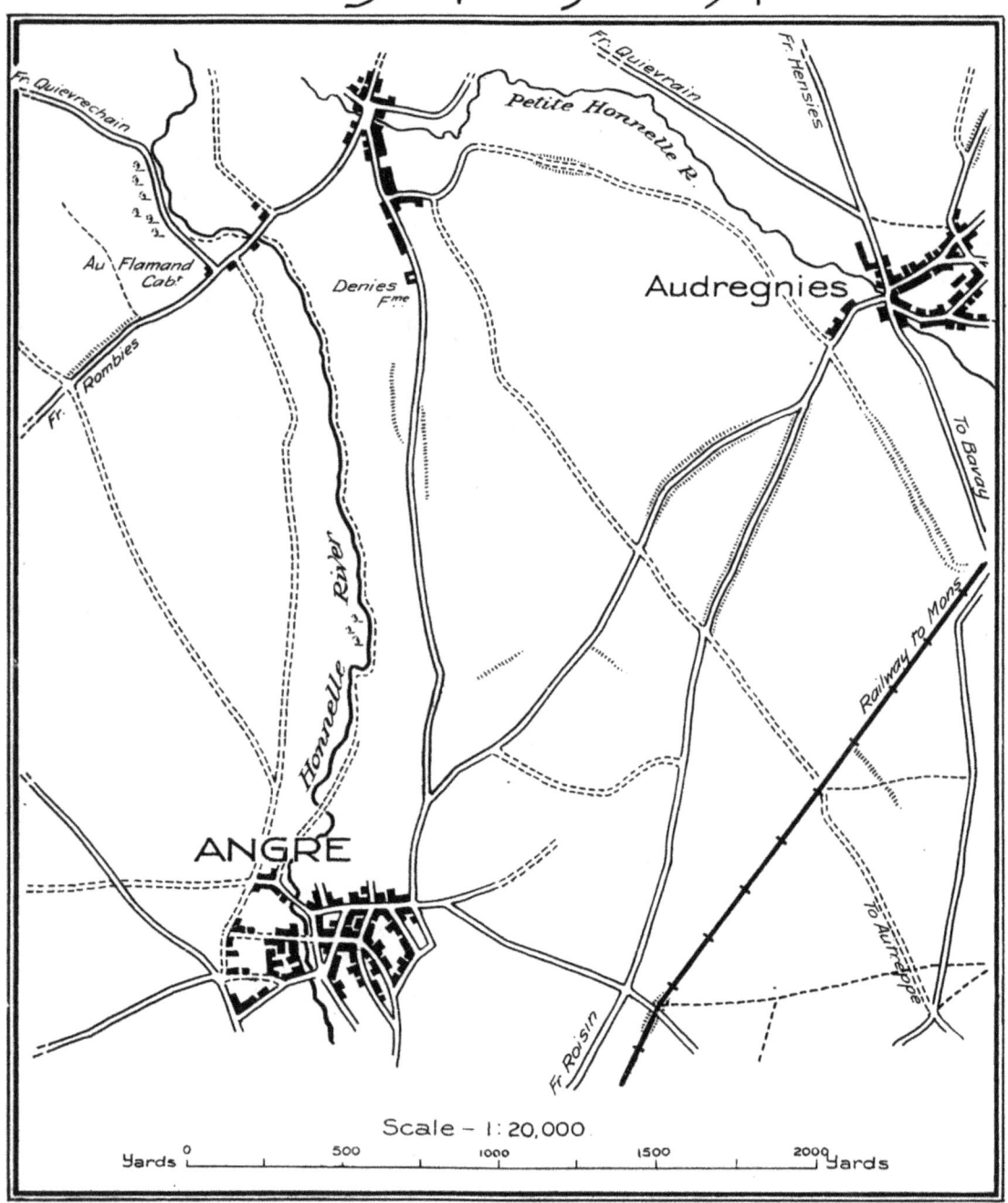

WESTERN THEATRE OF WAR

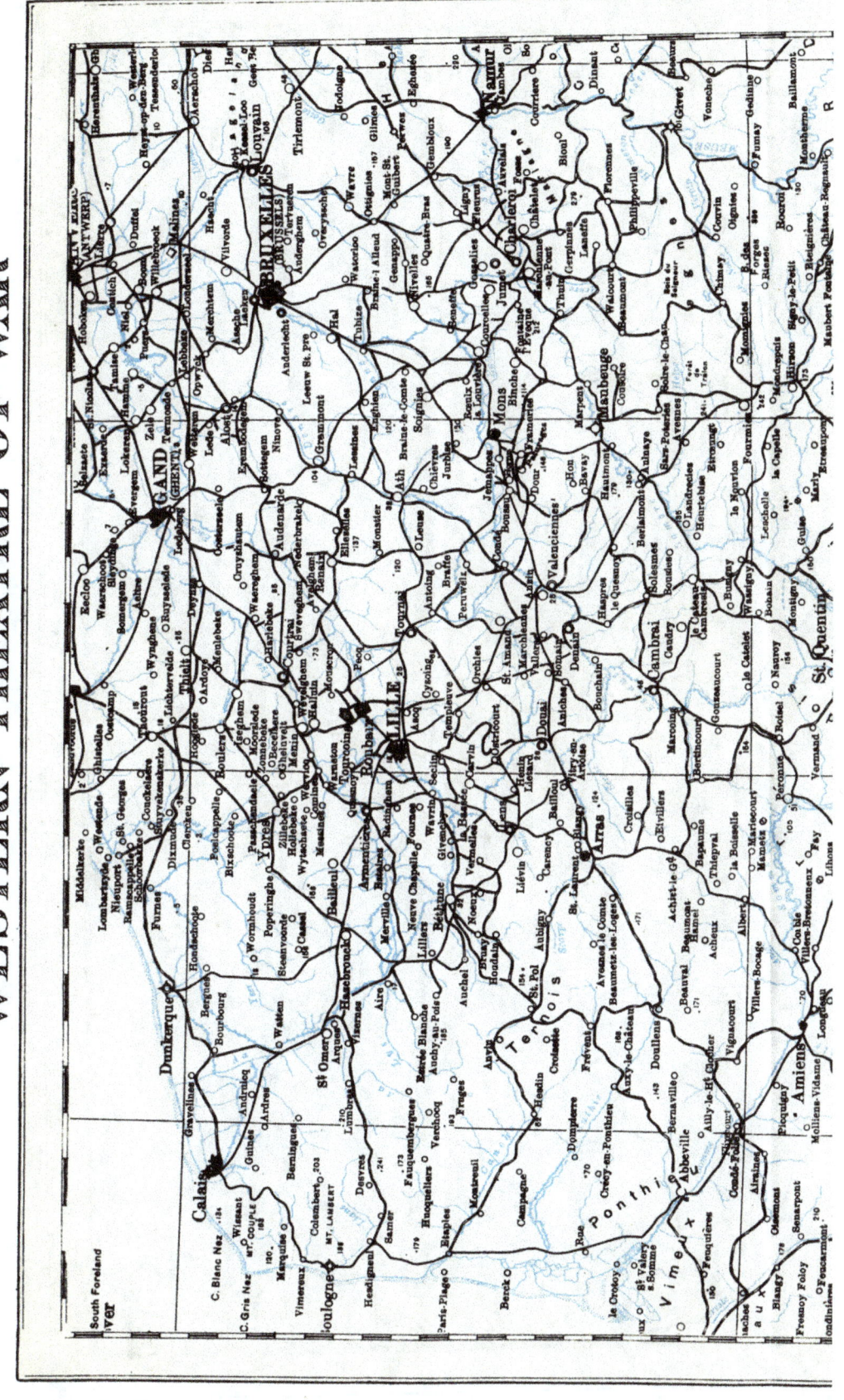

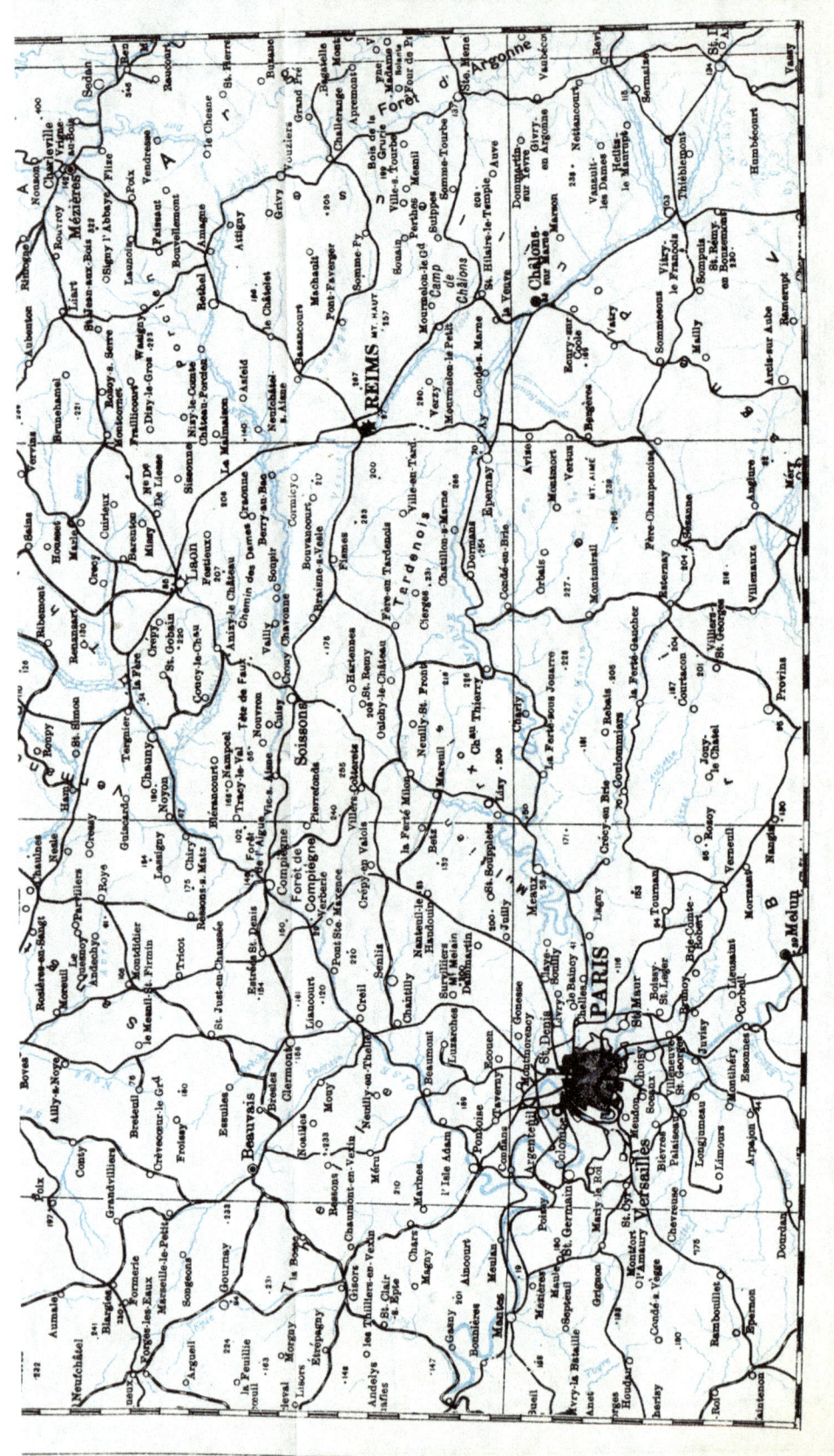

4th (Queens Own) Hussars

COUNTRY

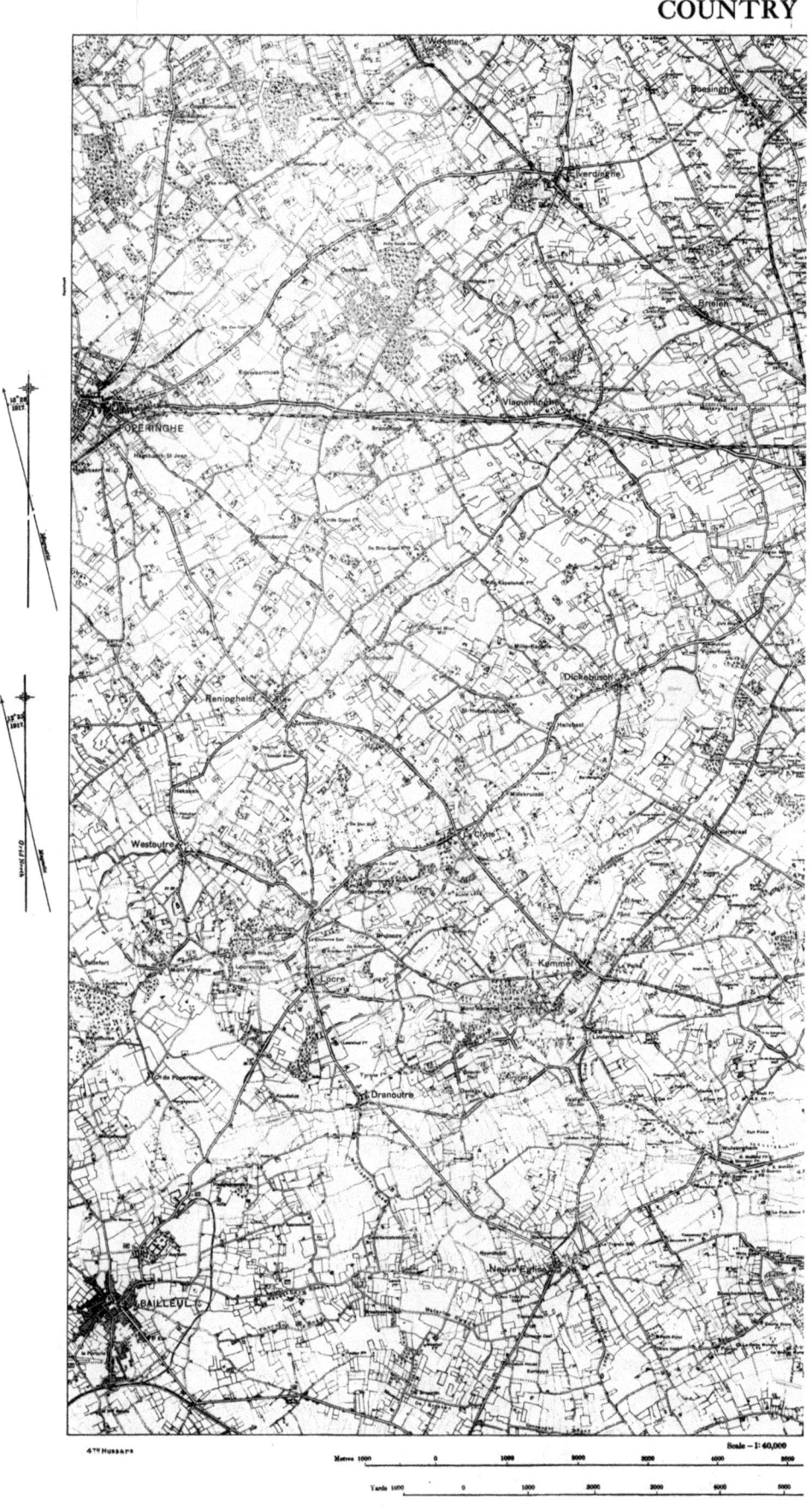

ROUND YPRES

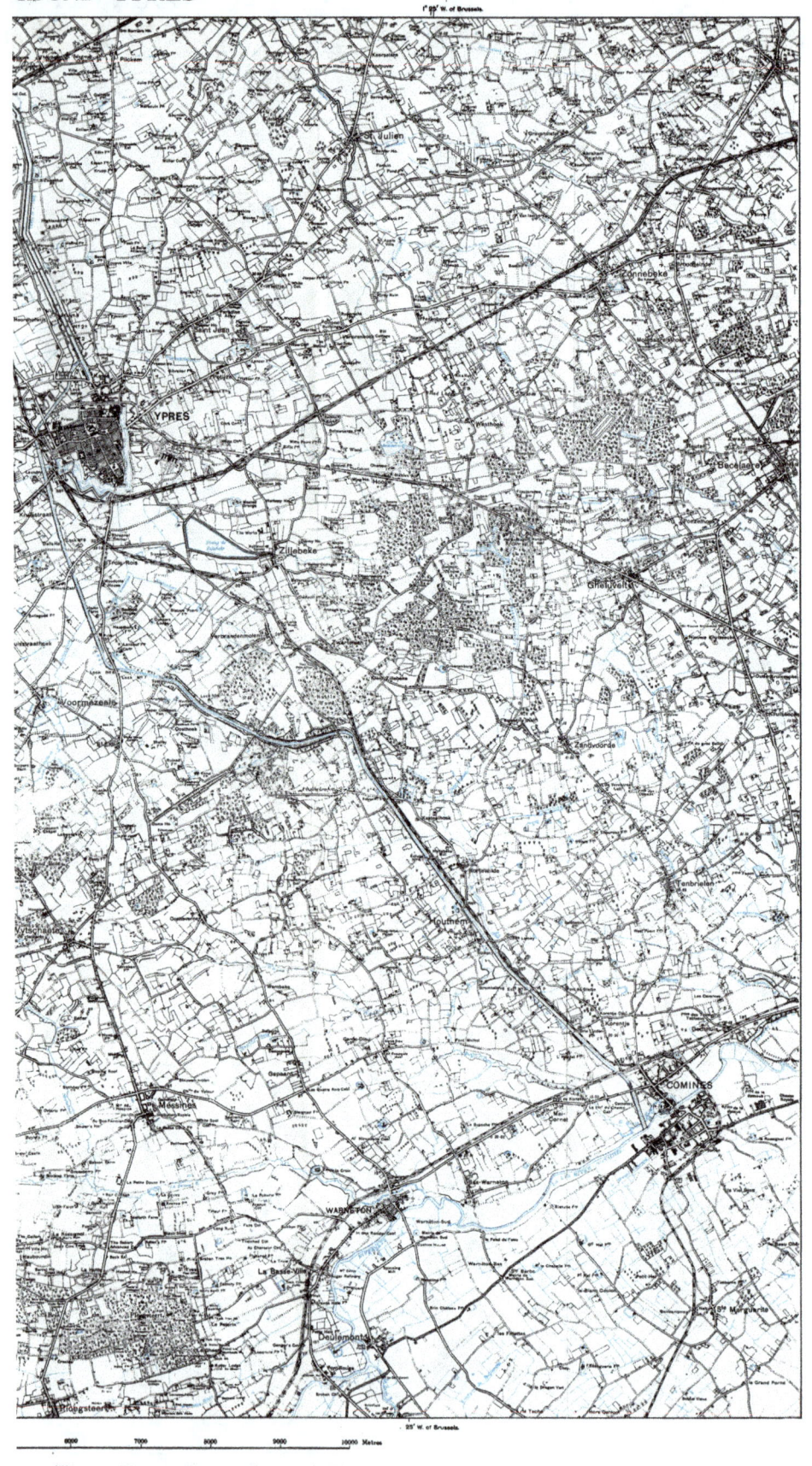

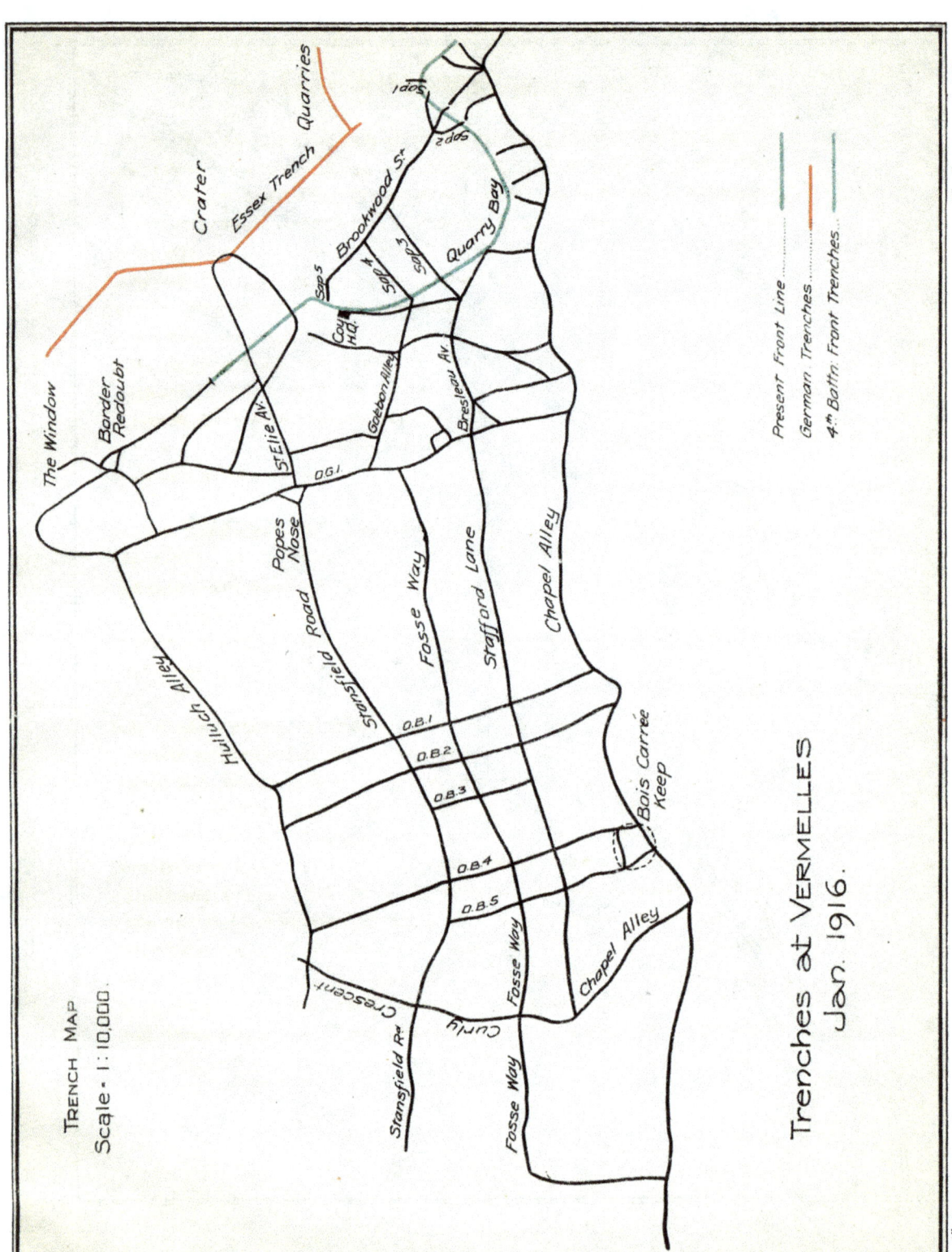

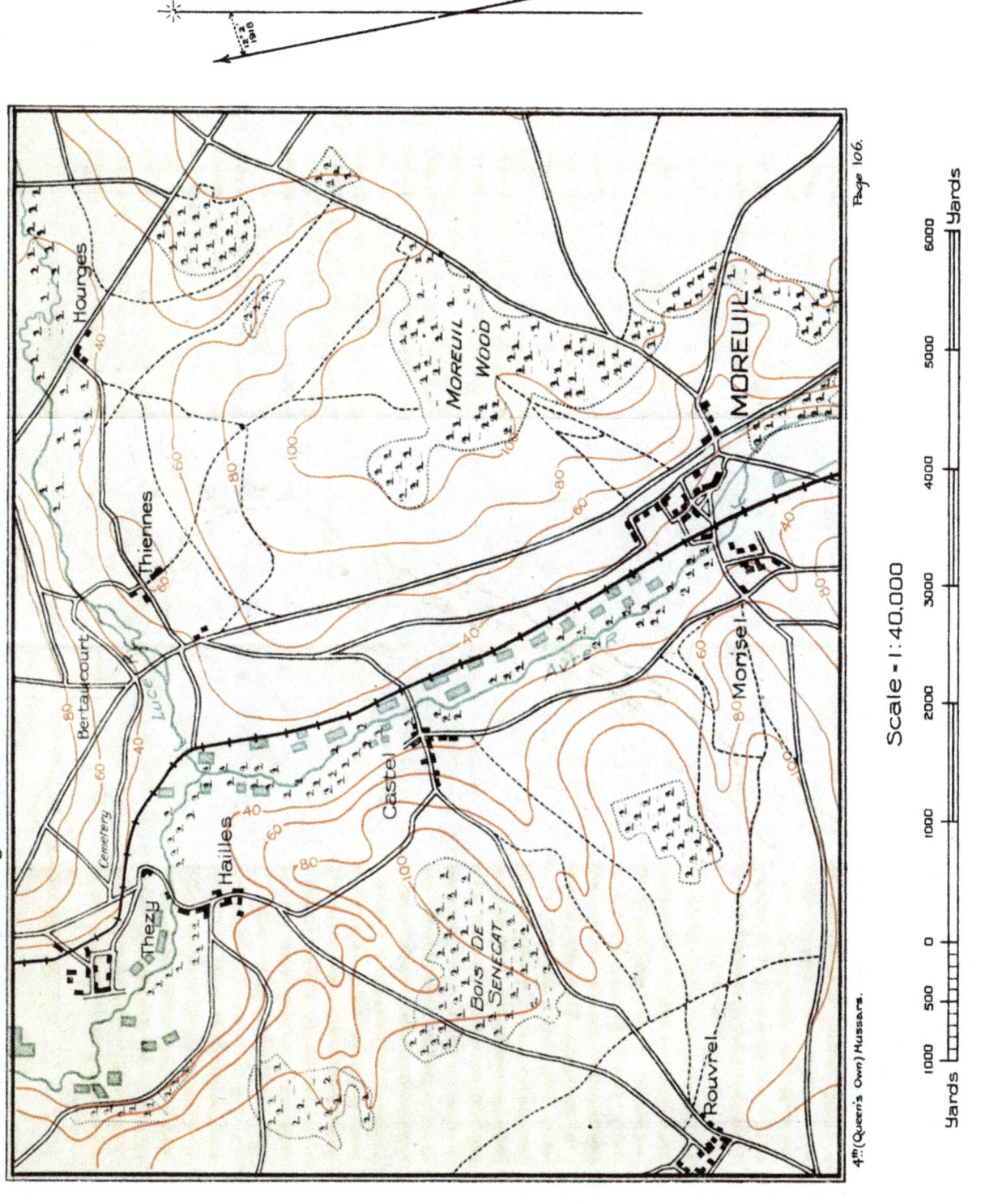

30th March to 1st April 1918.

THE 4th (QUEEN'S OWN) HUSSARS IN THE GREAT WAR

CHAPTER I

MOBILIZATION—ARRIVAL IN FRANCE—THE RETREAT FROM MONS.

4th Aug., 1914. On 4th August, 1914, mobilization commenced, and was completed by the 10th August. It went very smoothly as far as the officers and men were concerned, but the horses were a source of much trouble. Previously we had had eighty horses "boarded out," and, owing to the time of year, it was found that most of them were very unfit and a certain number unsound. The deficit had to be made up by drawing upon a large pool of requisitioned horses on the Curragh racecourse. We drew the full number the first day, and tried them at once under saddle. It was at once found that many were practically unbroken, others full of vice; but by a process of elimination, returning failures and drawing fresh ones, we were by the 10th fairly well mounted.

The men required to bring the regiment to a war footing were all reservists, either 4th or 8th Hussars, while we were fortunate in securing the attachment of one officer from the 8th Hussars and three from Indian cavalry, on leave in England. (*See* Appendix H.)

The 11th, 12th, and 13th were passed in drilling men and horses.

On the 14th the regiment marched by road to Dublin, arriving there on the 15th, where it embarked on the same day on the

THE 4TH (QUEEN'S OWN) HUSSARS

s.s. "Atlantian," a roomy cargo boat which had been hurriedly fitted out to convey horses. The regiment was commanded by Lieutenant-Colonel Hogg, Major Howell Second-in-Command. "A" Squadron was commanded by Major Darley, "B" Squadron by Captain Pragnell, "C" Squadron by Major Mockett. Lieutenant North commanded the machine guns, Lieutenant King being signalling officer. (*See* Appendix H for nominal roll of those embarking.)

16th Aug. The ship started at 4 a.m. on the 16th, and after a calm and uneventful voyage, escorted by a destroyer for part of the way, arrived at Le Havre at 7 a.m. **18th Aug.** on the 18th. After disembarkation, while still on the quay, an unfortunate incident occurred, "C" Squadron horses stampeding, and several horses being killed. These losses were made good from a remount camp, and by 9.30 p.m. the regiment had successfully entrained in two trains. Our French interpreters joined here—one officer and thirteen other ranks, most of whom, however, left us during the course of the retreat.

The first train started at 1.45 a.m. on the 19th, and arrived at Maubeuge at 7.30 p.m. on the same date, the second train being two hours behind.

All the arrangements for embarkation, disembarkation, and for the journey by train were alike admirable, while our French allies gave us a most enthusiastic and moving reception at the numerous stations *en route*. From Maubeuge the march was resumed by road the same night, French sentries in the environs of the fortress showing some suspicion of the unknown body of troops, an airship all the while circling in the sky above.

Billets that night were in Cousolre and Bersillies L'Abbaye, outposts being thrown out to the north on the report of the possibility of enemy cavalry patrols being in the neighbourhood. The 20th was a rest day, the maps issued giving most of the troops the first hint as to where they were likely to be employed. In the foggy morning of the 21st the 3rd Cavalry Brigade, which included ourselves, the 4th Hussars, the 5th and 16th Lancers, and "D" and "E" Batteries of the R.H.A., marched in a northerly direction, the destination being the village of Bray. These regiments and "D" Battery R.H.A. remained in the 3rd Cavalry Brigade to the end of the war. With the original Expeditionary Force was one Cavalry Division of 1st, 2nd, 3rd, and 4th Cavalry Brigades, and one detached brigade—the 5th Cavalry Brigade. Rumours were abroad of the existence of enemy patrols in the vicinity, but none were encountered.

The entire brigade billeted that night in Bray, each regiment being responsible for the protection of its own billets.

The country we had now reached was open and undulating, and though there were wire fences round the villages it was, on the whole, an admirable country for cavalry. This holds true of all the country we operated in during the retreat and up to October, 1914, though where streams or rivers occurred they were a very serious obstacle, as they were almost invariably bordered by strips of wooded marshy ground, impassable for mounted troops except at the bridges. There was much plough, but it had a good stubble on it, and was not bad going except after rain. Large woods do occur, but not often, and they may be seen on the maps.

22nd Aug. At 6 a.m. the brigade moved out to the high ground north-west of Bray, "A" Squadron 4th Hussars, under Major J. E. C. Darley, taking over the outpost line at Maurage from a squadron of the 5th Lancers.

During the morning a German aeroplane came over low—the first hostile aeroplane encountered—while an excited Belgian peasant brought news of a German Army advancing from St. Vaast.

Patrols from "A" Squadron soon encountered enemy patrols, which retired on being fired on. At noon "A" Squadron was withdrawn somewhat, and two strong patrols, under Lieut. Heyman and Lieut. Sword, were sent to Maurage and Boussoit respectively to watch the crossings of the River Haine, with orders to remain out till 5 p.m. These saw several hostile cavalry patrols, Heyman's patrol knocking over several men, first blood thus being drawn by the regiment. In the afternoon a serious enemy infantry attack developed on our right against the 5th Cavalry Brigade, the village of Peronne being at once set on fire, a sight striking enough at that time, but soon to become too familiar. The 16th Lancers took some part in this fight, and German field guns then shelled us lightly, the Brigadier, General Gough, having a narrow escape.

At 5.10 p.m. orders were received from the brigade to march to Elouges as soon as all detachments were in, and the brigade moved off about 6 p.m. over a country intersected with roads running through iron foundries and coal dumps, making it a very difficult matter to find the way after night fell.

However, the billets were reached at 4 a.m. on the 23rd, and we remained there all that day and till 4.30 a.m. the next morning, there being several false alarms during the night, all day and night fighting going on for the canal. On this date (24th) the brigade moved out to a ridge west of Elouges, whence a fine view was obtainable of the fight for the canal line. At 7.30 a.m. a retirement was ordered through Baisieux to Angre, where the regiment watered and fed. Scarcely had this been completed when the Cavalry Division received a message from the 5th Infantry Division requesting them to attack the enemy who were pressing their west flank. Within a quarter of an hour, at 12.30 p.m., the whole division was launched to the attack. The 4th Hussars were directed to gallop and seize the spur between the Honnelle and St. Pierre rivers running out towards Baisieux. "C" Squadron were ordered to line the north edge of the little wood half a mile north-east of Angre, while "A" and "B" Squadrons galloped across the enemy's front until reaching a sunken road running from Onnerjies to Baisieux, where they dismounted, sent the horses back up the ridge, and prolonged the right of "C" Squadron

24th Aug.

as far as the sunken road. While crossing in front of Baisieux, " A " and " B " Squadrons were under an intense rifle and machine-gun fire from the village, and a good many horses and one or two men were hit. The regiment remained in action here for two hours, keeping up a heavy fire on the Germans, who were trying to work up the St. Pierre stream, inflicting considerable losses on them. The guns meanwhile did great execution on the enemy advancing up the Honnelle River in massed formation. The regimental machine guns, under Lieutenant North, were in action with the other machine guns of the brigade on our left, and also did much execution.

At about 2.30 p.m. we were ordered to break off the action and retire, which was accomplished with great difficulty owing to the very heavy fire. The regiment suffered some 85 casualties, and had about 45 horses killed and wounded. All the wounded who were unable to ride had to be left on the ground, there being no means of conveying them; they fell into the hands of the enemy. Luckily some ten bicycles were found in an estaminet, which helped out the shortage of horses. Private Taylor, of " A " Squadron, was shot through the head here, and declared by the medical officer to be dead, and it was not for several months that he was reported a prisoner.

During the whole of the retreat this difficulty of evacuating wounded was experienced. There were few motor ambulances, and regiments were never in touch with what there were. The same remark applies to the horse ambulances in a lesser degree, and they were also too slow moving to pick up and convey wounded in a hurried retreat.

Both in this battle and subsequently Captain Wetherell, the regimental medical officer, showed great devotion to duty, attending wounded men under heavy fire, and being quite indefatigable. Sergeant Cox, R.A.M.C., was equally conspicuous for his complete disregard of danger.

The retirement was carried out under shell fire through the

THE 4TH (QUEEN'S OWN) HUSSARS

Bois Caillouquibique to Roisin, where much of the division reformed. The regiment moved on at 5.30 p.m. to Wargnies le Grand, where it held an outpost line in conjunction with the 19th Infantry Brigade. No supplies were received, but the country was full of oats, cut but not harvested, and from now on the horses never went short.

With this exception, rations and forage during the retreat and advance were almost invariably issued by the A.S.C., M.T., in what appeared to be a miraculous manner. Even thus early in the war the A.S.C. had little to learn about their job.

25th Aug. At 4 a.m. on the 25th patrols were sent out to Bry which scattered a Uhlan patrol, and at 5 a.m. the regiment marched to Verchain, the brigade doing flank guard to the Cavalry Division. At that village we passed a French territorial brigade, which was destroyed by the Germans later in the day. There were rumours amongst the inhabitants of German patrols in the vicinity and of large forces near Haspres, where heavy shelling could be seen.

Meanwhile hostile aeroplanes were constantly overhead, and at Point 94 shell fire opened from the west; moved to shelter of hollow east of Point 94; moved over Ridge 90, coming under shell fire again, which caused four casualties. The regiment got out of sight near St. Martin Farm, while the rest of the Cavalry Division again massed east of Maison Rouge and were again shelled. From the point of view of the regimental observer most of this day seemed to be spent in massing to form a target for enemy artillery, being scattered, and then forming up again.

The 3rd Cavalry Brigade now moved to the north-west of Vertain, where it halted until 5 p.m., when it crossed the Harpies stream and passed north of Vertain. While halted north-west of Vertain, a long column of troops was seen moving south on a parallel road some mile and a half to the east; this was taken to be a French force, but we were soon disillusioned, for, on reaching the Le Quesnoy road, rapid gun fire opened on the regiment from the east. This caused some casualties and not a little confusion, and two troops of " C " Squadron and one of " A," and including Major Mockett, Captain Brooke, and Lieutenants Cripps and Greville, became separated from the regiment, and were not seen again until the 29th at Chauny. Major Mockett did not rejoin then, and a month after it transpired that, after a series of adventures in disguise behind the German lines, he succeeded in reaching Dunkerque, though wounded. Privates Marney and Hensler also were dismounted, and succeeded in escaping after spending some time behind the enemy's lines.

Captain Scott took over command of " C " Squadron. On crossing the Le Quesnoy road, the regiment happened on a small depression in a cornfield, where it halted for twenty minutes. The machine-gun limbered wagon was hit, and half a limber had to be abandoned, the guns being extricated by the exertions of Lieutenant North and the personnel of the machine guns under heavy shell fire. While in the depression General Gough came up, and was at first for charging the enemy guns, but a personal view from the edge of the depression showed them to be securely behind several wire fences. All this while the shell fire was intense, but high and over, so that the regiment luckily got away with comparatively few casualties.

After this the brigade retired through Le Cateau to Catillon, where it billeted, guarding the bridges over the Sambre Canal, as we were not at that time in close touch with any troops on our east.

26th Aug. In the early hours of the 26th there was very heavy machine-gun and rifle fire in the direction of Landrecies, but we were not molested. At 6 a.m. the regiment moved off, after handing over the bridges to Scots Greys, who had by this time gained touch with us.

At Basnel the brigade came into action as right flank and rear guard to the 5th Infantry Division, and moved slowly through Baudival Farm and St. Souplet to Busigny, where a halt was made for two hours. During the course of the morning some view was obtained of the main infantry action which from our restricted point of view appeared to be going very favourably. At 2 p.m. the brigade massed for an attack on a reported Uhlan Brigade, which, however, failed to materialise.

At 5 p.m. we watered in Busigny, and then marched via Marety-Premont to Montbrehain, having some difficulty in keeping clear of a long mixed column, the débris of the battle of Le Cateau. At Montbrehain a halt was called from 10 p.m. to 1.30 a.m.

By this time, as may be imagined, men and horses were dead beat, so much so that it was no uncommon thing for men to go to sleep in their saddles, while after a short dismount it took at least ten minutes to get the men awake and on their horses.

At Montbrehain an order was issued to lighten the horses as much as possible, and greatcoats and one blanket were discarded.

27th Aug. At 1.30 we moved on, and on reaching Essigny telephoned through to St. Quentin to ascertain if the Germans had occupied it, intimation having been received, apparently from an official source, that the British Army was surrounded. We then went on to Homblieres, expecting to find German cavalry across our line of retreat at any moment. However, nothing was seen of them, though a false alarm was caused by a scarecrow in a field which many people were convinced was a Uhlan, so much was everyone feeling the strain caused by lack of sleep.

A halt took place here for four hours, when the brigade concentrated at 10 a.m. and remained concentrated until 2.30 p.m., owing to a report of a German column moving on St. Quentin. We finally went into Urvillers to billet, and there horses and men got a much-needed night's rest, fortunately finding a batch of newly baked bread in the village bakery.

28th Aug. At 10 a.m. on the 28th the regiment moved out south-west and halted, forming the rearguard to the brigade. During the course of the morning heavy firing could be heard to the north, and by 1 p.m. several hostile patrols were sighted and driven back by rifle fire, after which orders were received to retire to Benay at once, Captain Gatacre, with one troop, being thrown out to the right to connect up with the 5th Cavalry Brigade, which was about to be attacked. At 2 p.m., while the latter were heavily engaged, Captain Gatacre charged half a squadron of the enemy, putting them to flight and killing or wounding three himself.

At 4.30 p.m. we went into billets at Faillouel, the 16th Lancers finding the outposts, and at dawn capturing an officer of the 4th German Hussars. The regiment then took over rearguard and marched south, reaching Villequier Aumont at 11 a.m.

29th Aug. During this morning we received information from the brigade that, owing to a battle then in progress to the north, an advance might be ordered at any moment, but nothing came of this; while at 1.30 p.m. it was reported that a regiment of enemy cavalry and 700 infantry were a few miles north, advancing from Ham. As the regiment was about to retire, it was suddenly attacked by cavalry and infantry from the wood north of us, but after a brisk action the enemy was beaten off, having lost some men and horses, while we lost one man. Corporal Sharpe stalked a Uhlan in the wood, and ran his sword through him.

"B" Squadron remained south of Villequier Aumont watching the village, while the remainder billeted in the northern end of Chauny. The troops which had been missing since the 25th, having been working with the 1st Corps during this time, rejoined us here. They brought with them a message conveying the thanks of the 1st Corps for the work they had done while with them. At 3.30 a.m. the regiment crossed the Oise, bridges being blown up everywhere.

30th Aug. During the 30th we marched via Pierremande and Morhain to Nouvron, and billeted there, seeing no

THE 4TH (QUEEN'S OWN) HUSSARS

31st Aug. enemy till the morning of the 31st at about 9 a.m., when the regiment turned out on receiving information of thirty enemy cavalry. Only one or two were seen and shot, but in the afternoon a whole regiment was viewed, halted and dismounted some 1,500 yards away. They had apparently no one out, and we were preparing to attack them, but, unfortunately, a signaller using a flag from a haystack was seen by them, and they disappeared. At 4 p.m. we left Nouvron and crossed the Aisne towards Chelles, but on the way the Brigadier met a car from G.H.Q., some officers in which warned him of a very large German force advancing through Compiegne, and we thereupon went into billets at Roye St. Nicholas.

1st Sept. At 4 a.m. on the 1st September we marched through Mortefontaine to Taillefontaine, where we halted until 9 a.m., when hostile cavalry, infantry, and guns debouching from Roye St. Nicholas opened fire, "A" Squadron being heavily shelled, but only having one man and horse hit. The brigade then retired through the forest to Vex, "A" and "C" Squadrons being left to hold a mile front on a ride in the forest, with orders to hold on until 12.30 p.m., the object of the brigade being to fill the gap between the 1st and 2nd Corps. The enemy attacked through the forest in great strength, and at 12.30 were in many places right up to our line through the dense undergrowth. Colonel Hogg, who was standing up endeavouring to get "C" Squadron out of action, was badly wounded, and left in a house in Haramont with the medical officer, Captain Wetherell. They were both taken by the Germans that night, and Colonel Hogg died three days later, and was buried in the cemetery there.

Meanwhile the regiment rejoined the rest of the brigade and marched to Thury, arriving there at 8 p.m. Major Howell now was in command; Major Darley, Second-in-Command; Captain Pragnell, "A" Squadron; Captain Blood, "B" Squadron; Captain Gatacre, "C" Squadron. Lieutenant MacCallum joined

IN THE GREAT WAR

here for duty; he was appointed galloper to the Commanding Officer.

2nd Sept. At 3.30 a.m. we marched slowly via Acy-Nogeon Farm, Barcy, to Villenoy, which was reached at 8.30 p.m., the rearguard being driven in by shell-fire during the afternoon, but without becoming seriously engaged. This night orders were issued to march south-east, covering the movement of the British Army, which was moving in that direction to connect up with the French 18th Corps.

3rd Sept. In consequence, we moved at 4 a.m. to Penchard, thence to Barcy and Vareddes, where we halted some time. A German patrol was sighted here, but would not come on, so at 11 a.m. we withdrew to Germigny, and then to Montebise Chateau, where we billeted. The horses were very tired by now, and suffered from worn-out shoes, which could not be replaced owing to lack of supplies.

4th Sept. At 6 a.m. on the 4th we marched to Grand Glairet, where patrols reported the enemy crossing the Marne at La Ferté. We continued to Le Fayet, and halted there until 4.30 p.m., when enemy field-guns opened on us from Doué Hill. An artillery duel ensued in which our horse artillery appeared to get the worst of it, but the German shooting was rather wild and did little damage. We then retired to Montigny and went into billets, forming an outpost line in conjunction with the Black Watch.

5th Sept. On the 5th we marched at 4.15 a.m. to the concentration point south-west of Coulommiers. The regiment, with four guns, was detailed as rearguard to the 2nd Infantry Division, but did not find them till 11.30 a.m. in the Forêt de Crecy, having previously met one of their battalions which had lost touch with the remainder. A halt was made at the Chateau de Lumigny until 3 p.m., when we went on to Richebourg Farm, near Vilbert, finding our echelons there for the first time

THE 4TH (QUEEN'S OWN) HUSSARS

since 25th August. They were very welcome, as they had a certain amount of spare kit and much-needed horse-shoes.

And so ended the retreat, leaving the regiment much below its establishment, but still anxious to take the offensive. The regiment now consisted of :—Headquarters : Major Howell, Captain Darley, Captain Evans, Lieutenant King, Lieutenant MacCallum (an old 4th Hussar, who joined us on the 1st Sept.), and 15 other ranks. " A " Squadron : Captains Pragnell and Houston, Lieutenants Greville, Radclyffe, and Sherston, and 75 other ranks. " B " Squadron : Captains Blood and Brooke, Lieutenants Falkner and Heyman, and 84 other ranks. " C " Squadron : Captains Gatacre and Scott and Lieutenant Cripps, 73 other ranks, 2 cyclists. Machine guns : Lieutenant North and 18 other ranks. Total : 18 officers, 265 other ranks, including 4 interpreters. In addition to the above, who were all fighting men, we had 36 men with sick horses and the echelons.

Many points of administration and training were brought out during the retreat. Signalling was scarcely ever employed, as it was found too slow in this rapidly-moving warfare. Orders were conveyed by dispatch rider, being usually conveyed from Commanding Officer to squadron leaders verbally by the Adjutant. Orders from the brigade were conveyed by motor cycle, except when given verbally by the G.O.C. to Commanding Officers. Telephones were never used owing to lack of time.

IN THE GREAT WAR

CHAPTER II

THE ADVANCE TO THE AISNE—BILLETS IN BRAINE

6th Sept. On the night of 5th September a general advance was ordered, and in consequence " B " Squadron was detailed as a reconnoitring detachment to march to Marles at 6 a.m. the next morning, and report as to whether the Forest of Crecy was occupied by the enemy.

On arriving at Marles on the morning of the 6th, patrols were sent out to reconnoitre the forest, and found it full of the enemy, and several combats between opposing patrols took place, accompanied by some shelling, notably on Pezarches. The country was so thickly wooded that, beyond finding that the forest was held, no further information was to be gained.

Meanwhile the remainder of the brigade was kept concentrated east of the Bois de Lumigny, and at 5.30 p.m. moved forward through Lumigny to Pezarches without opposition, and the regiment was then sent to billet in Touquet, where we passed a quiet night.

7th Sept. At 8 a.m. on the 7th the brigade concentrated at Paradis, the 16th Lancers shortly becoming engaged near St. Augustin. There was some shooting on the part of German stragglers in the woods. The brigade then advanced, the regiment, with two guns, acting as advanced guard.

At Tie hostile shell fire opened, but did no damage, and our guns silenced the enemy artillery.

During this day we got frequent views of long columns of the enemy retreating in the distance, but our horses were still very tired and incapable of determined pursuit.

THE 4TH (QUEEN'S OWN) HUSSARS

North of Montigny there was some skirmishing in the woods, but at 1.15 p.m. we advanced on the bridges at Aulnoy and Martroy; we were held up at the former, but secured the latter at 2 p.m. The enemy was holding all crossings with machine guns at the bottoms of valleys, and was very difficult to dislodge, as our artillery could very rarely get a shoot at them.

After getting across at Le Martroy, we advanced towards Taillis, though the crossings to right and left were still held by the enemy. Lieutenant Cripps was sent forward to reconnoitre Les Marches with his troop, and was attacked there by infantry and machine guns from Taillis. He held on to the village, and was supported by "A" Squadron until the Germans withdrew from Taillis at dark, when he billeted there, the remainder of the regiment going to Chantareine.

There was no food left in the villages, the enemy having eaten everything and looted the houses, some of which were in a state of indescribable filth, resembling pig-sties. Quite a number of our men suffered from colic here owing to eating unripe apples.

8th Sept. At 5.40 a.m. on the 8th the brigade concentrated at Les Marches, and then marched to Mauroy, where we halted to let the 5th Infantry Division through us to attack the crossings over the Petit Morin. Here the remainder of the brigade was heavily shelled from across the river, "D" Battery R.H.A., which had been pushed right forward to shell enemy infantry on the far bank, being practically destroyed.

From here we moved to Le Plessier to wait until the infantry should have taken the crossings, and here we remained until 4 p.m., when we went into billets at Grand Glairet. The Germans then retired over the Marne, blowing up the bridges. This afternoon we passed General Sir John French and his staff, and from them learned of the great victory then being won on the Marne, which had the effect of heartening the troops immensely. That night it rained for the first time since the beginning of the war, we having been extremely fortunate as regards the weather up till then.

9th Sept. At 5.30 a.m. on the 9th the brigade concentrated at Perreuse Chateau, and remained there all day watching the French from the west and the British from the south shelling the retreating German columns north of La Ferté.

At 4.30 p.m. we marched through Jouarre and billeted in Les Feucheres.

10th Sept. On the 10th the advance was resumed at 4.45 a.m., the regiment forming the advanced guard to the brigade through La Platrière to Dhuisy, where the 15th Infantry Brigade were in action. Up till then "B" Squadron had been in front, but here the direction of march was suddenly changed to Premont, and "B" Squadron were lost and not picked up again till the afternoon. A large German column was sighted moving east, and our guns came into action against them.

Owing to the sudden change of direction, we became somewhat mixed up with the 5th Cavalry Brigade, but advanced to Premont. On arriving above Gandelu, we found it held by the Germans, which had caused the 5th Cavalry Brigade to pass to their right, thus clearing our front. Lieutenant Sword was found here, having been shot while patrolling. He had been sent out early in the day by "B" Squadron, but had gone much farther than was intended, and his patrol was fired on at close range from a wood. Several of his men were also hit.

The regiment attacked the village dismounted, and were in possession by 1 p.m., the enemy disappearing into the woods. We then mounted and pushed on, finding that the 5th Cavalry Brigade had swung back again across our front, and were engaged mounted and dismounted with the retreating enemy, as a result of which 1,000 prisoners and some guns were captured, our infantry also co-operating on the east.

THE 4TH (QUEEN'S OWN) HUSSARS

There was much débris lying about, and we took a pay-wagon containing some £30 in mixed coinage and some good maps with various artillery ranges marked on the former line of the German advance. The regiment joined up here with the remainder of the brigade, and we went into billets at Molloy, which had been very thoroughly looted by the Germans.

11th Sept. At 5.15 a.m. on the 11th we marched to join the brigade at Blangy, and we then advanced rapidly on Vierzy, where inhabitants reported some German infantry. They could not be located, and the advance was resumed to Villemontoire. From here the Germans could be seen entrenching the ridge at Noyon, and moving south-west from Soissons. At 2 p.m. heavy firing broke out to our north-west, which turned out to be French colonial troops mopping up a body of the enemy near Chaudun, and making some very pretty shooting with their 75's. The brigade stopped the enemy's escape on the east, and the whole appeared to be accounted for. The regiment then billeted in Villemontoire, two whole squadrons finding shelter in a large farm there.

12th Sept. At 5.15 a.m. the next day the regiment was detailed as flank guard to the brigade through Burgancy to Ecuiry. The going was very heavy owing to rain, and the advance delayed owing to the guns having to go through Royieres. There were still small parties of enemy holding the line of La Crise, and a good many stragglers in woods, one of whom fired two shots at Major Darley at a range of two or three yards and missed him.

"A" Squadron took the crossing at Ecuiry, Lieutenant Sherston's troop running into some of the enemy beyond it and having some casualties.

From a point south of the stream a good view was obtained of this fight, and a squadron of German lancers was also observed, waiting apparently to attack us on crossing the stream. They, however, cleared off without fighting. The French were very

heavily engaged all this time on our left. Our guns eventually got across at Royieres and joined the regiment, which then advanced to Ciry and found the brigade there.

At 2.30 p.m. the advance began into the Aisne valley, leaving " A " Squadron as left flank guard. A party of the enemy was located in a wood north-east of Chassemy, and the 4th Hussars sent down the road through Chassemy to get round their right. Chassemy was found to be lightly held, but was soon cleared, and the advance continued until half a mile beyond the village, when the enemy shelled us in column of route from across the valley. We turned east off the road and attacked the Chateau of Chassemy dismounted, which was taken by Captain Gatacre with " C " Squadron at 2.30 p.m., some cavalry being driven off. The rest of the brigade in the meantime took 100 men prisoners in the wood mentioned above.

At 4.45 p.m. Major Howell sent the following message to the brigade, giving the situation of the regiment :—

" Gatacre's squadron (' C ') comfortably established north end of wood near bridge with two maxims. Bridge appears to be intact, and is only about 500 yards from Gatacre. Uhlan patrols attempting to cross have been driven back and, except few men cut off and still wandering about woods, I doubt if any Germans S. of river in this quarter. Section of guns north of river spasmodically shelling Gatacre's troops and road through woods thence to Chassemy. Have two men (Mr. Burrell, the R.S.M., one) wounded in Chassemy, and should be glad of doctor or ambulance if available.

" Have lost the squadron you detached as flank guard (Pragnell). Do you know where he is ?"

The action of the regiment in thus preventing the enemy from crossing the Vailly bridge probably accounted for a good many enemy being cut off and captured on that and subsequent days. The regiment, less " C " Squadron, then billeted in Chassemy.

THE 4TH (QUEEN'S OWN) HUSSARS

13th Sept. On 13th September a halt was made while the various crossings over the Aisne were reconnoitred. The bridge at Condé was for some reason believed by the higher command not to be defended. As a matter of fact, it was very strongly held by machine guns and was not taken for many weeks. Lieutenant Cripps was sent to reconnoitre it at dawn, when he had a man shot; nevertheless, he was sent out twice more, each time losing casualties from machine-gun fire across the bridge; and finally an officer of the 5th Lancers was sent out, who disappeared.

The remainder of the regiment remained in their positions of the night before and rested, the enemy putting in an occasional shell and knocking out a battery of guns near by.

14th Sept. On the morning of the 14th, at 6.15 a.m., the brigade assembled at the chateau gates for an advance across the Vailly bridge. The 5th Cavalry Brigade crossed first, and at once came under heavy fire of all sorts, so that the hillside was dotted with the grey horses of Scots Greys. Crossing was impossible, so the 3rd Cavalry Brigade turned into chateau grounds again. At 12 noon we were ordered to retire to Courcelles and billet there. While our transport was still in Chassemy, the enemy shelled the column, and we had some casualties. The regiment turned off the road and moved under cover to Brenelles, thus probably avoiding further losses. On arrival at Courcelles, it was found full of First Army Headquarters, so we went into billets at Monthussard Farm, getting in very late.

While coming out of Chassemy the machine guns of the regiment, which were in those days carried in limbered wagons, had a very hot time from shell fire, but escaped without damage.

15th Sept. On the 15th "B" Squadron and the machine guns marched at 4.30 a.m., followed by the remainder of the regiment at 6 a.m., to Ancienne Wood, south of Chassemy, to demonstrate against the Condé bridge. The object of this manœuvre was somewhat obscure, but it was presumably intended to show the Germans we were in some strength there, and to prevent them from launching a counter-attack from across the bridge. While there a false report got about that the Germans had crossed the Aisne somewhere. During this and subsequent days such rumours were common, and may very probably have been spread by enemy agents. It was interesting to find between the Vesle and the Aisne a farm with English occupants. With characteristic British stubbornness, they refused to evacuate it, though it must inevitably have been destroyed before long.

At 5.30 p.m. the regiment was withdrawn, leaving "B" Squadron to watch the Condé bridge, their horses being in Chassemy. They were obliged to move their billets owing to shelling, but had no casualties.

16th Sept. On the 16th we received orders to turn out at 5 a.m., but these were cancelled, having been caused by another false report; but "A" Squadron went out to relieve "B" Squadron. On arriving opposite the Condé bridge, they were shelled and obliged to seek the shelter of the trees along the Vesle. They returned to billets at 5.30 p.m. The next day was spent in billets in Braine.

18th Sept. On the 18th the regiment marched out at 5.30 a.m., and remained in woods south of Chassemy all day, "C" Squadron being left out at night, the remainder returning to billets at dark, finding the Medical Officer, Captain Wetherell, who had been captured on 1st September, but had been left behind by the Germans when they retreated. He had many interesting tales to tell of the Germans, but had been well treated. R.S.M. Burrell and S.S.M. Dunsby both received commissions at this time for their conduct in the field.

19th-29th Sept. From 19th September to the 29th we remained in billets in Braine, getting our first real rest since the beginning of the war, with the result that most people got very fat.

THE 4TH (QUEEN'S OWN) HUSSARS

On the 24th we got our first and second reinforcements in one party, with them Lieutenants Levita and Schuster; they had been all over the country for some time unable to locate us. The party was 90 men, 129 horses. Three very good horses of the Percheron type were bought in the village, two of which went through the rest of the war, and after the Armistice were transferred to the 10th Hussars.

Captain Stokes joined on the 26th, having been on the way to Africa on a shooting trip when the war started, and finding a telegram of recall on his arrival at Capetown. He took over command of " B " Squadron. Captain Hunt, of the Indian Cavalry, also joined us here, as did a mysterious Frenchman—Dumont by name—who volunteered to come along with a motor. Permission to take him was granted by the brigade on condition the French authorities could vouch for him. An officer therefore went back to Paris with him, where the police identified him, and he returned with his Mercédès. He was with us until the 28th October, and the car was of enormous use. On that date he was summoned to the French mission at G.H.Q. and placed under arrest as a suspect. It was subsequently found he was partly of German extraction, and he spent the rest of the war in a French infantry barracks. His car we managed to retain until July, 1915, when it was impounded as unauthorized transport.

The casualties up to this date are shown in Appendix K. All through the retreat we suffered many more casualties in horses than personnel; this was largely due to the lack of horse-shoes, although we started with two spare shoes in the shoe-case. It must be remembered that every horse sick or unable to march meant a man out of action, for there were no fresh supplies of horses to draw on. We were therefore considerably weaker in fighting strength than would appear from the number of casualties.

While in Braine the regiment collected a large number of stragglers from other units, many of whom had not seen their units since the early days of the retreat. It speaks well for the discipline of the old Army that these men had advanced with other units than their own rather than be left behind when the Army advanced.

On the 24th September squadron parade strengths, which included first and second reinforcements, were "A" 104, "B" 102, "C" 106, all including officers, so even with reinforcements the regiment was much under strength, and required to complete— officers, 2; men, 150; riding horses, 150; bicycles, 11. The loss in bicycles was large, and was chiefly due to troops moving across country during the retreat. The cyclists during this period and throughout the war did very good work, and were of great assistance in carrying messages from Headquarters to squadrons by day and night.

While at Braine the first issue of bayonets was made, and in time every man carried one. They proved of great moral value especially when trench warfare set in, though never actually used on the enemy by the regiment.

On the 27th September Lieutenant-Colonel Bridges, D.S.O., from the 4th Dragoon Guards, arrived to take over command of the 4th Hussars.

Our period of rest ended on the 29th September, the horses being in good condition again, with the exception of those which arrived with reinforcements. We had also been completed in officers, but not in men, being still 150 short.

The original Cavalry Division was split up here. The 1st and 2nd Brigades formed the 1st Division, the 3rd, 4th and 5th Brigades the 2nd Division, commanded by Major-General Gough. Both Divisions formed one Cavalry Corps, under General Allenby.

CHAPTER III

FROM THE AISNE TO THE FIRST BATTLE OF YPRES

30th Sept. to 10th Oct. Now began the long, flanking march by the British Army which was destined to end at Ypres. The 4th Hussars left Braine on the 30th September, and marched north, moving in the evenings, by the following route:—Cuiryhousse, Tigny, Oigny, Bethisy St. Martin, Tricot, Domart, Frémont, Montigny, Monchy to Berguette, which was reached on the 10th October.

On the 3rd October Colonel Bridges left the regiment, going off in a motor-car to G.H.Q. We learnt afterwards that he was bound for Antwerp for liaison with the Belgians. His knowledge of Belgium was extremely valuable at this juncture, and his subsequent career was a brilliant one.

10th Oct. The first news of the enemy was obtained on the 10th October, when we were informed that French cavalry had been in action about the Forêt de Nieppe. Our march on that day was therefore a " war " march, with the 4th Hussars as advanced guard, with orders to take over the crossings of the Lys Canal from the French. French detachments were found on the canal crossings, but the main portion of their cavalry appeared to be all west of the Forêt de Nieppe, following on an action of the day before about Vieux Berquin.

The regiment went into billets in Berguette, as they were ordered to relieve the French the following day. A suspected spy was arrested in the village and handed over to the brigade.

IN THE GREAT WAR

11th Oct. On the morning of the 11th the 4th Hussars took over the bridges from the 30th (French) Dragoons, and put them in a state of defence. At 1 p.m. "B" Squadron was sent to St. Venant, to reconnoitre the Forêt de Nieppe and east of it. They saw only one or two patrols near Vieux Berquin, but the inhabitants said there was German cavalry about.

At 5.30 p.m. we assembled at Isbergues and marched to Steenbecque, billeting there with an outpost line along the railway to the east. Our "B" Echelon did not reach Isbergues till dark, and from there took the wrong road, marching through the Forêt de Nieppe, well outside the outpost line, but arrived safely without encountering any enemy.

Oct. 12th The brigade marched at 6.15 a.m. on the 12th October in a very thick fog, the 4th Hussars in rear. Slow progress was made, but the 16th Lancers took Borre and reconnoitred the Mont des Cats. At 10 a.m. the fog lifted, and the 4th Hussars took on advanced guard to Caestre, which place was evacuated by German cavalry as we came up. Two troops of "C" Squadron, under Captain Gatacre, were now detached to act as escort to the R.H.A. battery on Hill 55.

At 1.30 p.m. the 4th Hussars was ordered to advance through Flêtre and reconnoitre Meteren, the remainder of the brigade being directed on the Mont des Cats. Flêtre had just been evacuated, but on advancing towards Meteren our patrols were soon fired on, while artillery also opened fire on the southern edge of Flêtre from somewhere east of Le Coq de Paille. Captain Hunt, with the remaining two troops of "C" Squadron, seized the farms on a ridge half a mile east of Flêtre. He sent Lieutenant Dunsby out to endeavour to locate the hostile guns, and he spotted a German observing from a tree. He succeeded in getting right under him, when the German dropped right on him, half stunning him. The German then stood over him and tried to blow his brains out, but only hit his cap. Lieutenant Dunsby

23

was not clear as to what happened to the German officer after this, but he went off, and Dunsby succeeded in walking back.

The farms meanwhile were held by Captain Hunt, with patrols out, while some sniping went on. He was withdrawn at dark, at which hour the ridge west of Meteren and Meteren itself were still held, apparently by infantry, who stopped our patrols from advancing.

Outposts were put out round Flêtre that night with barricades on all roads. The situation was then—5th and 16th Lancers on Mont des Cats; Lieutenant Falkner and one troop at Le Coq de Paille; our infantry on line Borre to Strazeele; 1st Cavalry Brigade about Merris and Vieux Berquin.

Meanwhile Captain Gatacre had been ordered to reconnoitre Mont des Cats in the morning shortly after being detached with two troops. He advanced up the slope south of the hill, and dropped part of his two troops there below a small wood. The enemy had not shown themselves up to this point. He then went on with Lieutenant Levita and a patrol up the road which skirted the hill, and then turned up over the hill just north of the monastery wall. The Germans allowed them to advance almost as far as the monastery wall, and then shot them both dead at short range. The remainder of the patrol retired on the two troops. The loss of Captain Gatacre was a very great one, for he had proved himself an exceptionally gallant officer.

During the subsequent attack and capture of the hill by the 5th and 16th Lancers the two troops of the 4th Hussars, under Lieutenant Cripps, rendered valuable assistance from their position half-way up the hill, killing many of the enemy. Lieutenant Cripps and some seven or eight men eventually entered the monastery with the 16th.

Captain Hunt took over command of " C " Squadron. Prince Max of Hesse was killed here, and almost every man of the brigade who was engaged on the hill claimed to have shot him.

IN THE GREAT WAR

13th Oct. At dawn on the 13th a German patrol rode right into Lieutenant Falkner's troop at Le Coq de Paille. They wounded and captured one, belonging to the 8th Jaegers. At 7 a.m. the farms occupied by Captain Hunt on the previous day were reoccupied by him. Meanwhile patrols had gone out at dawn to reconnoitre Meteren, and found it occupied. They remained in observation. A fine view of what followed was obtained from the church tower in Flêtre. A troop of German cavalry emerged from Meteren and followed our patrol in, in column of route mounted on the road. An ambush was hurriedly laid, a machine gun being placed commanding the road, and some dismounted men were also put out. A patrol of ours rode in quietly past this, followed by the Germans. When the latter were within fifty yards, the German officer halted, drew a pistol, and fired two shots. Our men opened fire, the machine gun jammed, and the whole German troop went " files about " and galloped down the road. Their escape was almost incredible, but it was some consolation to the observers on the church to see two or three fall from their horses before reaching Meteren.

At 10.15 a.m. the brigade advanced from Nooteboom on our left, and advanced east until the 5th Lancers were held up on Hill 68. At 11.45 a.m. the 4th Hussars advanced and joined hands with the 5th Lancers on Hill 68. Here they halted until the rear squadron (" C ") came up. The enemy were found to be holding some farms and woods south-east of Point 68. The 5th Lancers were attacking these, our " B " Squadron, under Captain Stokes, co-operating. They made some ground, and this brought the brigade into close contact with the 1st Cavalry Brigade, so much so that " B " Squadron were cut off from the regiment by the Bays. They were withdrawn back to the regiment, and just after they had passed the Bays, at about 3.30 p.m., the enemy delivered a counter-attack with a battalion against the left of the Bays and the 4th Hussars. The Bays and " B " Squadron,

THE 4TH (QUEEN'S OWN) HUSSARS

4th Hussars, were driven in somewhat, but the enemy's advance was then checked, and on some of our infantry coming up we advanced at about 5 p.m. against a large farm held by the enemy. The latter, however, did not stay to fight, and we got a good target of their retreating columns at about 700 yards' range.

During the German counter-attack Lieutenant Lonsdale was mortally wounded, and several men of " B " Squadron, among them Corporal Bowstead and Private Temple and Private Bennett, showed great courage in bringing him out of action in a wheel-barrow, the two last named being wounded while doing so. Lieutenant Lonsdale's death was a great loss to the regiment, for he was a most promising and fearless officer.

As soon as dark fell we were withdrawn and sent to billet in Godewaersvelde, where we found large numbers of French Territorials, and got in with some difficulty. The French troops seemed to have very little idea as to what they were there for, and several times during this early part of the war we came across similar bodies of French Territorial troops, all seemingly very busy, but apparently without any particular mission, or even under the administration of any higher formation. This night Lieutenant Greville was detailed for a long patrol—to find the Headquarters of the 7th Cavalry Brigade in Ypres and carry dispatches to them. It was a particularly unpleasant job, for it meant going some twelve miles through country reputed to be full of enemy patrols and possibly larger bodies.

14th Oct. At 7 a.m. on the 14th Lieutenant Greville set out, and as a matter of fact reached Ypres without encountering any enemy, meeting some of the 7th Cavalry Brigade on the way.

The remainder of the regiment marched at 11 a.m. as advanced guard via Boeschepe and Reninghelst to La Clytte, where we met the Royals. We then turned south-east over the saddle of

Kemmel Hill to Neuve Eglise, seeing only small patrols of the enemy, retreating at the gallop. The 18th Hussars were holding Neuve Eglise, and there was some shooting going on between them and some Germans in the wood south of the village. The regiment was ordered to seize and hold Wulverghem until relieved by the 1st Cavalry Brigade. We found no enemy there, but there was a Belgian armoured car there pierced with bullets and burnt out. We were to go to Lindenhoek when relieved, but by 7 p.m. no other troops had arrived, and we therefore billeted in Wulverghem, with outposts on all the roads. We had now reached the Flanders district, where on the flats the roads were bounded by deep muddy ditches, unjumpable by horses, and we were thus almost entirely confined to the roads. A more unsuitable country for cavalry it would be hard to find.

During the night a fire broke out in a farm occupied by a post of " B " Squadron, and as a Death's Head Hussar busby was found there, it looked very much as though the owner of the headgear had been hidden there, and set fire to the place and slipped away as soon as it grew dark. This night was very foggy, as were many nights about this time.

15th Oct. At 7.15 on the morning of the 15th the brigade assembled at the cross-roads one and a half miles north-west of Messines, and advanced through Messines, the 16th Lancers doing advanced guard, who found Warneton, Pont Rouge, and Frelinghien all held by the enemy. Meanwhile the 5th Cavalry Brigade advanced north of us and pushed on to attack Comines, which was held by the enemy.

At 1 p.m. there was a good deal of shooting to the west of Warneton, and the 4th Hussars were sent forward to clear up the situation and to support the 16th Lancers. " C " Squadron reached the 9th kilometre stone at Garde Dieu. From there an attack was organized on the north-east corner of Warneton, and a farm seized at the level crossing near the town. We were then ordered to withdraw and entrench a line through Gapaard and round the base of the Messines Ridge. Squadrons were disposed as follows :—

    1st Squadron—Farm one-third of a mile south of d of Gapaard ; small farm one-third of a mile south-west of F of F^{me}.

    2nd Squadron—Farm and cross-roads.

    3rd Squadron in reserve north of 2nd Squadron.

Then all began to dig in, our Commanding Officer, Lieutenant-Colonel Howell, being one of the first cavalry officers to realize the extreme importance of the spade even to cavalry in modern warfare.

16th Oct. At 6 a.m. on the 16th a dismounted patrol was sent out by "A" Squadron into Warneton. They had two men killed at the barricade at the entrance to the town, the enemy firing from houses. The other squadrons also sent out patrols which drew fire from the town.

We were much troubled at this period by civilian refugees, for there were undoubtedly spies amongst them, while at the same time they could not all be ordered to return to the enemy's lines ; and, on the other hand, it was impossible to watch and control their movements after they had entered our lines. They brought, however, much useful information, especially as to the state of the bridges over the Lys Canal. The points of local interest on which they afforded information were that the enemy had destroyed the Warneton bridge, but were using the Pont Rouge, and that 1,000 of them had arrived the day before at Warneton, and a number of them had crossed to the left bank of the canal.

At about 10 a.m. we were ordered to advance on the north-east outskirts of Warneton and seize them, and to send a squadron to Bas Warneton to reconnoitre it, and, if possible, to occupy and hold it. "A" Squadron, under Captain Pragnell, was detailed for this duty, and moved off at 10.30 a.m. By 12.15 they were holding the railway crossing and farm on the Bas Warneton road, and patrols sent into the village were fired on ; but by 1.30 p.m. they occupied Bas Warneton, and established the machine guns there also. They could see the enemy busy digging trenches beyond the canal, and they appeared to have constructed four lines of trenches some hundred yards apart. The diggers were harassed with machine-gun fire at about 1,400 yards' range.

Sergeant Scotcher's troop of "C" Squadron had meanwhile been sent dismounted down the main road into Warneton, and established themselves, in the face of slight sniping, in the outlying houses of that village.

This was the situation at 3.30 p.m., when the brigade was ordered to seize the portion of Warneton lying north of the river. 4th Hussars were directed round by the north-east, 5th Lancers down the main road from the north, 16th Lancers from the west. All regiments were to meet in the Place. The object in view was not stated and was somewhat obscure.

"A" Squadron was ordered to hold on to Bas Warneton and the farm at the railway crossing. "B" and "C" Squadrons, with Headquarters, advanced dismounted down the road from the north-east corner of Warneton, and got without opposition to the main Warneton—Gapaard road. They also seized the station there. All the houses were opened *en route* and hurriedly searched. In the centre of the village was found a plate with what was evidently the sentry's dinner on it, still hot, so he had evidently left hurriedly. There were some scattered shots from all directions, apparently coming from houses; and when "C" Squadron advanced into the Place, they found the church and convent apparently strongly held, the enemy firing through shutters at close range, wounding two men. The 5th and 16th Lancers did not join hands with us till about 6 p.m., when it was growing dark. By this time the enemy appeared to spring up from their places of concealment amongst the houses, and firing grew quite brisk. The enemy were apparently firing straight down the street from across the bridge, and bullets were striking sparks from the *pavé* and walls as they came skipping along. The enemy also fired a house in the Place, which lit the town up with a lurid glare.

THE 4TH (QUEEN'S OWN) HUSSARS

They also fired some few heavy shells into the Place, while we were ordered to light up all the houses and make as much display as possible, presumably to impress the enemy with an idea of our strength and confidence. The whole scene was a remarkable one, and the Germans were by now firing from roofs in all directions, while our men broke into the houses and set lights in the windows.

It was rather an anti-climax after all this display to be ordered to retire from the town and Bas Warneton at 9 p.m. to Gapaard and Garde Dieu. This we did without any difficulty or casualties, and billeted in the most matter-of-fact way in the last-named villages. Meanwhile the Germans spent a very restless night throwing heavy shells into Warneton until the morning.

17th Oct. The next day a few civilians were seen about the houses north of Warneton, and then disappeared, and a short while afterwards parties of the enemy, with several machine guns, appeared about the same place, but did not advance beyond the village. The Brigadier expressed his appreciation of the very useful reconnaissance carried out by " A " Squadron in Bas Warneton the day before.

At 12 noon the regiment handed over to the 3rd Hussars, who were at once attacked, but not very seriously, and we went back to Wulverghem into billets, where the night was much disturbed by heavy firing in the direction of Ploegsteert.

18th Oct. The 18th was spent resting, squadrons being reorganized into three troops owing to the shortage of men.

That night intimation was received that the 7th Division would advance on Menin the next day, the 5th Cavalry Brigade protecting their right flank, the 3rd Cavalry Brigade to take over the position vacated by the 5th.

19th Oct. At 7 a.m. on the 19th the regiment marched via Wytschaete to Hollebeke, and after hanging about there all day, went into billets. " B " Squadron found the outposts—two troops near the lock, one troop just west of canal on the Zandvoorde road, one troop south of canal on the Ypres road.

IN THE GREAT WAR

CHAPTER IV

20TH OCTOBER—20TH NOVEMBER, 1914

FIRST BATTLE OF YPRES—HOLLEBEKE—WULVERGHEM—HERENTHAGE CHATEAU

20th Oct. On the morning of the 20th the regiment was ordered to entrench a line running through Hollebeke, and we were very busy digging, employing a good many civilians to help us and using civilian tools. The regiment was disposed—" B " Squadron astride the canal and railway just south of the Zandvoorde road, " C " Squadron round the south-east outskirts of Hollebeke, " A " Squadron round the south-west outskirts. We made the mistake in these early days of building overhead cover to the trenches, which made them far too conspicuous, as we were to learn on the 30th and 31st October.

At noon orders were received to prepare for a retirement in case the 5th Cavalry Brigade were forced in. There was some uncertainty throughout this period as to the position of other bodies of troops, and it was very rare to be informed of the movements of other units, which we had to find out for ourselves. For instance, in this case we were not informed where the 5th Brigade was, and were ourselves unable to locate it; it was not, therefore, easy to conform to their movements. Colonel Howell was, however, indefatigable in obtaining information as to neighbouring troops, and, thanks to his energy, the regiment was usually better informed than most as to the situation.

At 1 p.m. we were ordered to entrench the chateau east of the canal on the Zandvoorde road, and " A " Squadron were sent there. At 1.45 p.m., in consequence of the retirement of the 5th

THE 4TH (QUEEN'S OWN) HUSSARS

Cavalry Brigade to Oostlaverne, the regiment was ordered to cover this, and squadrons were moved into the following positions : " B " Squadron (two troops) to the cross-roads south-west of Zandvoorde ; " C " Squadron to the eastern exits of Kortewilde, connecting up with the right of the 7th Infantry Division. The remainder of " B " Squadron remained in Hollebeke, " A " Squadron in the chateau. Their orders were to remain out until the rear of the 5th Cavalry Brigade had passed through, retiring. Both the two troops of " B " Squadron and " C " Squadron were shelled at dusk, but only two men were wounded.

These dispositions left Hollebeke for the time being practically undefended, and the whole line held by the regiment was so long that a determined attack on any portion of it must have got through. At 5.80 p.m. most of the 5th Cavalry Brigade had passed through, but one squadron was still out, and this eventually retired without passing through us, and so it was not until 9.80 p.m. that we heard they were all clear. At that hour " C " Squadron was ordered to leave one troop dismounted watching Kortewilde, to keep touch with the 5th Lancers, the remainder returning to Hollebeke, as did Headquarters. Orders were issued for the following readjustments to take place at 5 a.m. the next day :— " B " Squadron (less one troop) to the chateau, there recall the Zandvoorde troop ; " A " Squadron from the chateau to the west end of Hollebeke ; " C " Squadron, centre of Hollebeke, recalling the Kortewilde troop ; one machine gun to the chateau, one to Hollebeke. At 11.80 p.m., however, the " C " Squadron troop from Kortewilde, under Lieutenant Cripps, having entirely failed to find the 5th Lancers, came in, and was kept in Hollebeke.

The orders and counter-orders, movements and counter-moves, on this day are given in some detail in order to show the uncertainty of the situation at this time. A general attack was expected, and we had not the troops to man the whole line. It was therefore necessary to move continually from one threatened point to another, which involved an immense amount of work for all ranks, and at the same time prevented our fortifying adequately our real position—*i.e.*, Hollebeke. It was probably extremely fortunate that the Germans were not ready to attack for another week, by which time the line was better organized and there were a few more troops up, though the line then was still woefully weak.

21st Oct. On the 21st all were expecting an enemy attack at any moment, while our situation was far from satisfactory, as there were apparently no troops between Hollebeke and Zandvoorde, and the position of the 5th Lancers was uncertain. As soon as it got light the situation began to clear up, and at 9.30 a.m. the 5th Lancers were astride the canal to our front at the lock and windmill. Our left was still in the air, so "A" Squadron, under Captain Pragnell, was ordered to Klein Zillebeke to fill the gap.

No sooner was he clear of the village than heavy field-gun fire opened on it. The first shells struck the Curé's house, just evacuated by Headquarters, and the estaminet was the next target, Lieutenant Cripps and a cyclist being wounded there. The firing increased, but was directed almost entirely against buildings in the higher portion of the village, and not at all against the trenches in front of it where our men lay. This was probably due to the care with which they had been sited by Colonel Howell, and to his strict orders against movement near them by day. The 5th Lancers now withdrew from our front, and German infantry began to advance from Kortewilde, some crossing the canal and advancing along the west bank, while cavalry were seen farther to the east. There was probably a whole brigade of German infantry advancing along both sides of the canal by 11 a.m., and "B" Squadron and one machine gun, and especially one advanced troop, under Captain Brooke, had some fair targets, though the country was rather blind. Our gunners were put on to some targets, and did some execution; while the 6th Cavalry Brigade guns, coming up north of the canal, near the Ypres road, were also given targets by us.

THE 4TH (QUEEN'S OWN) HUSSARS

This appeared to steady the German advance, and we were by 12.30 p.m. feeling pretty comfortable, and felt we had the situation well in hand, more especially as 100 cyclists had now filled the gap on our left, when we were ordered to retire, first to the canal bend north of Hollebeke, and then towards St. Eloi. The withdrawal was gradually carried out, the enemy showing no great desire to press on in face of our fire, and by 2.30 p.m. we were just clear of the village. At this juncture counter-orders were received, to hold on to Hollebeke at all costs. The regiment immediately turned about and went forward to occupy its former positions. On reaching the village again, however, it was found that the enemy had occupied the chateau and the houses level with it, west of the canal. At 3.30 p.m. we arranged, in conjunction with the 10th Hussars on the east of the railway, to attack the chateau. The 10th Hussars, however, did not attack, and the Germans advanced from it instead against our " B " Squadron, covering the canal and railway crossings there, and by 4.15 p.m. the attack was becoming serious. However, the Germans shot remarkably badly; we got our guns on to them, and this, combined with our rifle fire, caused their attack to die away at about 4.45 p.m.

At 6.30 p.m. the situation was much the same, the 10th Hussars having been told to occupy the chateau if not held by the enemy. They sent patrols down, who apparently reported it held. Meanwhile our patrols found the canal crossing evacuated, and " B " Squadron occupied it at 9 p.m., sending patrols also into the chateau, which was unoccupied. However, at 12 midnight the enemy, also finding it not held, reoccupied it, and from there made it too uncomfortable for our men at the crossing to remain there.

" A " Squadron had by now rejoined, and a squadron of Yeomanry held the bridge north of Hollebeke for a time, but then withdrew, and we sent a troop to hold it. It transpired afterwards that it was some shooting by our men at the crossing which led the 10th to believe the chateau held at 9.30 p.m. These shots were fired at a cow.

When the regiment arrived at Hollebeke, three officers of the 14th Hussars—Captains Mewburn and Mason and Lieutenant Moule—arrived for attachment, so we were better off for officers again.

22nd Oct. On the morning of the 22nd we were informed that the 6th Cavalry Brigade would attack the chateau and then hold it, but at 9 a.m. our patrols found it empty, and it was subsequently occupied by one squadron of the Royals. During the day 200 men of the Munsters came up to take over the chateau. Seventy of these were diverted to Hollebeke and came into our trenches, which were now becoming very strong. A platoon also held the crossing north of the village.

It should be explained here that from the canal bend north of Hollebeke down to Kortewilde the railway was on a high embankment, fully exposed to the fire of both sides. It therefore became a matter of extreme difficulty to maintain touch between troops on either side of it, patrols being shot at as they crossed.

Commander Samson came up in the morning with a 3-pounder gun on a lorry and an armoured train. We were able to give him some good targets at the enemy who were surveying and digging trenches 1,200 yards to our front. He was able to dislodge two German posts, one from a windmill and one from the lockhouse, and it was pleasing to see one German blown off the top of the lofty windmill. Commander Samson was a remarkable shot with his 3-pounder, but was somewhat of an embarrassment to us owing to his foible for wandering between the British and German lines. At 8 p.m. an attack developed somewhere on our right, and, as often happened at that period, the firing spread continuously, although the attack did not extend to our front and we did no shooting. One man of the Munsters got hit slightly by a ·303 bullet.

THE 4TH (QUEEN'S OWN) HUSSARS

23rd Oct. At 6 a.m. on the 23rd the 129th Baluchis arrived and relieved the 4th Hussars and the Munsters, and we went back to our horses, sent the day before to farms south of Verbrandenmolen and the shooting-lodge on the Ypres road. We left, however, ninety men in Hollebeke as a support, and also our machine guns, under Lieutenant North.

The armoured train came into action, with the result that a good many hostile shells were fired into Hollebeke, but luckily they were still aimed at the houses and farms, and none at our trenches. Meanwhile the regiment was very busy, with the aid of some civilians, digging a second line along the canal from the broken bridge to the railway line, and this work was continued until the 30th October, by which time the line was quite strong, having the canal as a good obstacle, the only weak spot being the railway, which prevented our co-operating well with the troops on our left.

24th Oct. On the 24th we received news that a general German attack was expected, and the 1st and 4th German Cavalry Corps were expected to attack the front held by our Cavalry Corps.

Enemy aircraft were busy observing, and the enemy could be seen digging 1,200 yards in front of Hollebeke.

During the day we found a mounted squadron, part of a composite regiment formed to co-operate with the 3rd Cavalry Division in a projected forward movement. Nothing came of this, and they returned in the evening. German snipers worked up at night and hit some Baluchis.

25th Oct. On the 25th our support in Hollebeke was withdrawn, and Captain Scott arrived with some reinforcements, Captains Egerton and Gannon and 125 men, all mounted.

In the evening, at the request of the Baluchis, the support again went up, and rejoined in the morning. This native regiment was wholly unused to European warfare, and depended very much on their white officers, and they were given to indiscriminate firing on the slightest pretexts.

Our fighting strength, with reinforcements, was :—Officers, 20 ; men, 288, with two machine guns and horses. When the horses were away, the dismounted men were reduced to 230, and this was our strength when the fighting really began on the 30th.

That night we were ordered to be ready at 1 p.m. to relieve the Baluchis with one squadron, to release them for attack, and to move east of railway with remainder, ready to attack. Machine guns to remain in position to cover Baluchis.

26th Oct. At 1 p.m. on the 26th " C " Squadron took over Hollebeke, and the Baluchis advanced, but made little progress. At 2 p.m. " A " and " B " Squadrons moved east of railway up behind the chateau, being shelled *en route*, the enemy firing on armoured train. The Royals in the chateau said they had orders to protect the right flank of the 3rd Cavalry Division in an attack on Kortewilde. At 3 p.m. " A " Squadron advanced past them and reached the outskirts of Kortewilde and the lock, meeting with little opposition. It was found impossible to communicate with the Baluchis the other side of the embankment, and it was not until that night that we found they had made very little ground, but had had heavy losses.

At 3.30 p.m. a staff officer of the 3rd Cavalry Division warned us their guns were about to shell Kortewilde. " A " Squadron was therefore withdrawn, having been entirely unsupported on either flank. Our brigade stopped this firing, and " A " Squadron went forward again, but found the lock held by men who said, " Come on, we are friends." Lieutenant Sherston, who spoke Hindustani, addressed them in that language, whereupon they opened fire, but missed in the growing darkness. This squadron, being still unsupported by any advance on either flank, was then withdrawn. We sent " B " Squadron also into Hollebeke, " A " Squadron back into billets.

THE 4TH (QUEEN'S OWN) HUSSARS

At 10 p.m. the Baluchis returned to the line they had started from in the afternoon, and "B" and "C" Squadrons also withdrew to billets.

27th Oct. At dawn on the 27th Corporal Ewens, who had twice reconnoitred the lock the previous evening, was sent out again. He found it held, and was fired on at ten yards' range, but escaped. He was afterwards awarded a decoration for these useful reconnaissances. At 6.30 a.m. we were ordered to relieve the Baluchis with 180 men, which was done. The day was spent by the remainder in very strenuous digging on the second or canal line. It was found when we took over Hollebeke this morning that the enemy had pushed trenches forward to 800 yards, and were sniping hard. They also shelled the village in the morning.

The next two days were spent in a similar manner, our billets being lightly shelled, and also bombed by aeroplanes.

30th Oct. The next morning, the 30th October, our troops in Hollebeke were relieved by the 129th Baluchis, and the regiment was ordered to report mounted to the 6th Cavalry Brigade at Klein Zillebeke. We reported there, and at 9.30 were asked by Colonel Bulkeley Johnson, commanding the composite brigade supporting the 6th Brigade, to attack in order to relieve him. Colonel Howell thereupon rode down towards the chateau, which had been reported captured by the enemy, but found this and its vicinity held by the 10th Hussars and Royals. At this time a heavy enemy attack commenced on the Zandvoorde Ridge, and they could be seen from just east of the canal, some of their field batteries galloping into action in the open over the eastern end of the ridge and firing somewhat wildly on our squadrons, which were at this time east of the canal. Heavy fire was also directed on the chateau. From this personal reconnaissance by Colonel Howell it was seen that the main enemy attack at this time was directed against the Zandvoorde Ridge, and this they occupied about 11 a.m. with infantry and guns.

IN THE GREAT WAR

Meanwhile it was difficult to know under whose orders exactly we were working. Within an hour conflicting orders were received from 2nd Cavalry Division, 3rd Cavalry Brigade, 3rd Cavalry Division, 6th Cavalry Brigade, and a composite brigade under Colonel Bulkeley Johnson. At 12 p.m. we were ordered by 2nd Cavalry Division to co-operate with the Greys and 3rd Hussars in a counter-attack on Zandvoorde, but the Greys and 3rd Hussars were not to be found. At the same time orders were received from 6th Cavalry Brigade to watch their right and support the chateau, and the latter was eventually done. At 12.45 p.m. orders were received from 2nd Cavalry Division to leave one squadron to support the right of 6th Cavalry Brigade, and report with the remainder to 3rd Cavalry Brigade. At 1 p.m. a message was received from Colonel Bulkeley Johnson to report to General Gough at Hollebeke. At 1.15 p.m. the situation was :—" A " Squadron, in response to a request from 6th Cavalry Brigade to support their right flank, which was being attacked, was occupying a trench between *petit* chateau and chateau vacated by 10th Hussars; " B " Squadron, as requested by Royals, was helping them to hold chateau; " C " Squadron was at the canal bend north of Hollebeke in reserve.

At this moment an order was received from 3rd Cavalry Brigade. This stated that the Baluchis and 5th Lancers had been driven out of their position in line with Hollebeke, and were retiring to the second line with their left on the broken bridge. The 4th Hussars were to endeavour to take over the canal line on their left, but only if it was not occupied by the Baluchis originally in Hollebeke. The latter could now be seen by us trickling out of Hollebeke under heavy shell fire and disappearing into the woods. It afterwards transpired that all their white officers were killed or wounded, their right left in the air, and they disintegrated entirely, and also inevitably, under the circumstances.

At 2.30 p.m. orders were received from 2nd Cavalry Division that the 4th Hussars were to be under General Vaughan (3rd

THE 4TH (QUEEN'S OWN) HUSSARS

Cavalry Brigade) alone, and were to report to him. Already, in accordance with the former message from 3rd Cavalry Brigade, the regiment had been withdrawn from east of the canal, and was now disposed—" A " Squadron about broken bridge, " B " Squadron railway to road crossing over canal, " C " Squadron holding the canal line between the two. The horses were sent into the woods some mile and a half in rear. By 2 p.m. we were safely installed in the trenches previously dug, and also previously allotted to squadrons and well reconnoitred by them; so that our line was now well organized, and we knew where we were for the first time during this very confused and busy day. No sooner were we in the trenches than a very heavy shell fire was directed on the left of this line. This line was a very strong one naturally. On the left between the railway and the road over canal the trenches ran along low ground in a fence; behind them a wooded hill ran up fairly steeply, and proved an irresistible attraction to the enemy gunners on this and the next day. Just to the right of the road, facing the enemy, rose a steep embankment, north of the canal, being the soil dug from the canal. This was covered with ten-year-old fir-trees. At the point where this began were the two machine guns and a troop of " C " Squadron. Their trenches were rather too obvious, and caught it badly the next day. The remainder of " C " Squadron were in narrow slits on top of the embankment, and were never spotted by the enemy, who fired either over or short, into the canal. On their right was a short gap, then came " A " Squadron in small narrow trenches covering the broken bridge and the woods of the white chateau. The latter were scarcely shelled at all.

All the morning and up to 2 p.m. Lieutenant North, with the machine guns, had been in Hollebeke. Messengers were sent to recall him then, and he came in about 2.30 p.m. He had been in action all the morning, and had stayed in Hollebeke an hour and a half after all other troops had left. With his two guns he had held up probably the best part of an enemy brigade, and when he got the order to retire the enemy were within 100 yards of him, and he got the most wonderful targets from 600 yards downwards, and must have done tremendous execution. He got his guns away in a wheelbarrow, and had only one man wounded, astonishing though it appears. This man, by the way, was too bad to move, and was left, and another man stayed with him. They were never heard of again.

By 4 p.m., though shelling was very intense and the Germans had brought up field guns into Hollebeke and were firing at 700 yards' range, the situation seemed much more comfortable, for everyone concerned apparently realized that at midday the canal had been unoccupied for a distance of about a mile, and began to send supports. Thus, the 3rd Cavalry Division said they were supporting us, and sent us a squadron of Life Guards. At 4 p.m. a message came from over the railway from Colonel Smith, commanding the Grenadier Guards, to say an attack seemed to be developing on the right, and asking us to hold the bridge with the French, so they were presumably somewhere about also, though we did not see them until the next day. This was the first intimation we got that the Guards were on our left, as we believed the 10th Hussars and Royals to be still there.

The 18th Hussars connected up with us on our right. During this day the artillery of the brigade fired pretty well their last round, and in any case their guns were about worn out.

Just before dark German infantry began to advance from Hollebeke, especially along the west side of the canal, which was covered with bushes. They were well sprinkled with bullets, and did not press home any attack this night. At 6.30 p.m. we blew up the bridge over the canal, though the girders of the foundation still held. Just after this we received orders not to destroy the bridge, as an attack was planned for French troops to carry out the next morning.

All through the night there was much singing and band playing by the Germans in Hollebeke and beyond it. The night was

THE 4TH (QUEEN'S OWN) HUSSARS

31st Oct. otherwise quiet, but at dawn on the 31st shelling started and grew heavier. This continued all day, and at times was very intense, but the damage was comparatively slight, the casualties on the 30th and 31st amounting to two officers killed, five men killed, and 21 wounded.

The officers were Captain Hunt and Lieutenant North. The latter had already been recommended for the D.S.O., and for his work on the 30th was recommended for the V.C. He had throughout the campaign displayed an absolute disregard of his personal safety, and on the 30th his conduct in Hollebeke, left absolutely in the blue with his machine guns, was heroic. Captain Hunt was killed by a second shell when extricating Lieutenant North after he was hit, in doing which he had to come out of cover. Captain Egerton took over " C " Squadron.

As soon as it was light on the 31st we could see by scrapes in the ground that the enemy's advanced scouts had been right up to the canal on the south bank during the night. Many of them were visible in the village, moving to the railway and woods round the white chateau. " A " Squadron were heavily sniped, but more than held their own at this game, and claimed to have hit a good many Germans.

At 10 a.m. the enemy shell fire became very intense, and they had by now got their field guns again firing from Hollebeke. " A " Squadron found it difficult all day to get messages through owing to heavy fire, and had several men hit while carrying dispatches; while the clearance of wounded could not be effected till dark, the rear of our position being so swept by shell fire.

About 11 a.m. the French on the east of the railway began to advance, but never really got beyond our trench line, being stopped by shell fire; they, however, remained close up.

At 3.30 p.m., after more intense shell fire, the enemy advanced in several waves from Hollebeke. He was met with rapid fire from " B " and " C " Squadrons, the machine guns having been knocked out during the morning, and his attack was brought to a standstill some 300 yards to our front. His losses must have been heavy, and he made no further infantry attacks this day. Immediately after this some French troops thickened our line, and two squadrons of Life Guards came up at the double, to find the attack already repulsed. Some French guns supported us during the day, and guns of the 3rd Cavalry Division, and they must have inflicted considerable losses on the assembling attacking troops.

During all our open fighting of the war, and in this battle in particular, it was found that much the quickest way of getting artillery support was to send a mounted officer direct to the guns with the target. This duty was usually entrusted to the Adjutant or some other officer on the regimental Headquarters, and it is well worth considering whether it would not be worth while to have an officer attached to regimental Headquarters whose only duty in open warfare would be to maintain liaison with the gunners. The latter have no officers to spare to be attached to regiments.

After dark we were ordered to hand over to the French and Life Guards, and to go to St. Eloi to billet, but to leave " A " Squadron where they were until the next morning. We marched to St. Eloi, but on going there to billet found the village under heavy infantry fire from medium range, and therefore moved to Voormezeele and bivouacked there, the houses being occupied already by other troops.

1st Nov. At 6 a.m. the regiment marched to Kemmel, while heavy fighting seemed to be going on between Wytschaete and Messines. At about 7.30 a.m. " A " Squadron rejoined, and we were employed in supporting our troops which were scattered (in a rather disorganized state owing to the fierce battle for Messines the night before) between Kemmel and Messines. The whole situation was very obscure, and could be cleared up only by personal reconnaissance. From Hill 75 the Germans could be seen advancing from Messines at 10.30 a.m., but they appeared to stop when fired on, and showed no determination, though the confusion in our lines was all in their favour. No doubt, though, they were in at least equal confusion, owing to the heavy losses they had sustained.

The regiment remained all day on the slopes east of Kemmel, putting a few posts out to fill gaps in the line to our front.

At dusk we were ordered to form an outpost line running through Hill 75. This was not, however, the British front line, which was some half-mile in front of us, composed of other brigades of cavalry, some native troops, and linking up with the French about Wytschaete.

At 12 midnight, however, the French took over our line, putting a thousand men in Wytschaete and to the cross-roads south-west of it, and having another five thousand somewhere in support. The regiment therefore went into adjacent farms for the night.

2nd Nov. At 5 a.m. on the 2nd the regiment was withdrawn to Kemmel, while the Germans, under heavy artillery fire from Messines, captured part of Wytschaete from the French. A French cavalry corps now arrived and counter-attacked, but succeeded only in checking any further enemy advance.

Meanwhile we dug a secondary line near Kemmel up to 2 p.m., when the 2nd Cavalry Division concentrated at Locre, there being some idea of an attack on Messines. This was abandoned at dusk, and we went into billets at Berthen. During this day Lieutenant Heinekey and forty-eight men joined from the Base.

Lieutenant King took over the machine guns, vice Lieutenant North, and Lieutenant Sherston became signalling officer, vice Lieutenant King.

3rd Nov. In the morning of the 3rd the brigade moved to the Croix de Poperinghe to support the 1st Cavalry Brigade, holding trenches east of Wulverghem. At 2 p.m. we moved to Dranoutre. At dusk we were ordered to leave our horses and take over the above trenches, dismounted.

IN THE GREAT WAR

In the dark, therefore, we took over a thin and very exposed line of trenches, already obviously thoroughly registered by enemy guns. There was some sniping, enemy crawlers getting quite close in the turnips.

4th Nov. At 11 a.m. on the 4th a French dismounted cavalry corps, under General Conneau, attacked through us, and brought heavy shell fire on our trenches. We therefore evacuated our centre front line and brought "C" Squadron back. This move was badly carried out, was spotted by the enemy, and they were shelled again.

The French were all over the place, and the situation was utterly vague, no one seeming to know what anyone else was doing. At 6 p.m. heavy rifle fire broke out to the right and left, so the front line was occupied again, while the Greys and 20th came up to thicken the line during the hours of darkness. Heavy rifle fire continued throughout the night on our right and left, but we got only sniping. The French appeared to have made no progress on our front, and could not be located.

During the day a shell hit and knocked over two hay-stacks, under which our regimental Headquarters lay in a trench; we were not seriously buried, however.

During this day and the next Interpreter Moreau was very useful, and showed great courage in effecting liaison between our right and the French, south of the Wulverghem—Messines road. The French there were in front of the 5th Lancers and echeloned to our own right front.

5th Nov. At 5.30 a.m. on the 5th the Greys and 20th Hussars withdrew. At 10 a.m. heavy shell fire came down all along the front, and continued until 12 noon, when the Germans advanced from Messines in dense columns and captured Hill 75 from the French, in spite of great efforts on the part of officers of the 16th Lancers to rally them. From our trenches we had a clear view of all the attack, and were able to furnish our guns with good targets, which, let us hope, led to heavy losses to the enemy infantry.

When the hill went we occupied our front line again, experiencing more losses from shell fire, which continued, with heavy rifle fire, till dark. At this hour the 5th Dragoon Guards relieved us with some difficulty, owing to the narrowness of the trenches and the heavy rifle fire.

These two days cost us thirty-seven casualties, amongst the wounded being Captain Mason, 14th Hussars. They were two very unpleasant days, as it was a case of sitting in very obvious trenches being shelled, without a chance of much retaliation. We then went to Berthen to billet there.

6th-12th Nov. From the 6th to the 12th November the regiment rested in Berthen, but were turned out more than once owing to critical situations arising on the front. At 11.20 a.m. on the 12th we were ordered to Neuve Eglise to take over some trenches. On arrival there it was found impossible to take over by day, while our assistance did not appear to be required at all. We therefore returned to billets. Captain Scott and Captain Long joined.

13th Nov. At 6.30 a.m. on the 13th we marched to Dranoutre, where the horses were left, and at 3.30 p.m. we went to Wulverghem, dismounted, taking over the same trenches as on 5th November. An interpreter and a sergeant were wounded by the same bullet on going into the line. We found that the Germans holding Hill 75 sniped a good deal from the flank, and also brought up a gun or guns quite close by night.

The weather had now turned very cold and wet, and we had a good deal of sickness, "trench foot" making its first appearance.

14th Nov. On the 14th we commenced digging a support trench, 200 yards in rear of the front line, but were stopped by shell fire at 4.15 p.m. The position of the French was still rather difficult to make out, but we gradually got some clear idea of the situation, which was almost precisely as we had left it on the 5th.

15th Nov. On the 15th work was continued on the line, but the weather was very wet and cold, and combined with sniping to make digging difficult. At dark the Oxford Yeomanry relieved us, and we marched via Neuve Eglise and an almost impossible road to billets about Nooteboom. Our machine gun wagons had a particularly hard time, getting bogged *en route*.

16th-18th Nov. From the 16th to 18th we remained in billets, Captain Clutterbuck and Lieutenant Christie joining us here.

19th Nov. We marched on 19th November to relieve the 1st Cavalry Division on the Ypres—Menin road east of Hooge. Started at 11 a.m. in snow and sleet, marched via Dickebusch and Ypres, and took over from the 9th Lancers after dark. The trenches were near a ruined chateau and stables, and were in very close contact with particularly aggressive Germans, who were supplied with a very heavy trench mortar which had tremendous shattering effect, and soon destroyed any trenches it was directed against.

It had now cleared up after everyone had got thoroughly wet, and the cold was intense; and since no fires were allowed, owing to the proximity of the enemy, and as there was no shelter, everyone suffered very much, wet clothing becoming as hard as boards. There was much sniping round the stable.

20th Nov. The next morning, when it grew light, some shelling commenced, and shortly after the trench mortar began.

By 9 a.m. the stable was much damaged and had to be evacuated, while the trench from the stable to the chateau was obliterated. Lieutenant Schuster was killed here by a sniper, and it was not till after dark that Captain Scott was able to get his body out.

When night fell the enemy occupied the stable, and an order was received at 7 p.m. that, if held, it was to be attacked, and then destroyed by the Royal Engineers. For this purpose we had some hundred men of the K.O.Y.L.I. to help. They had been in action continuously since the commencement of the battle of Ypres, and some of their men were in a very bad state owing to the continuous strain.

Colonel Howell pointed out that a night attack over that ground, covered with broken trees and débris, was not likely to succeed, and in any case field guns were necessary to reduce the stable walls. Captain Scott was then sent forward with his troop to reconnoitre the position. He found the stable occupied and a good many Germans about, and also found that the trench was flat. He was then ordered to dig this trench again with his troop, and set to work on it. The regiment was then ordered to attack and take the stable at all costs, but this was again cancelled. French troops came up at 9.30 p.m. and took over from us, the French commander agreeing with Colonel Howell that the stables were something of a death-trap, and were best left to the Germans.

On the way down the Ypres road the regiment was shelled and Captain Brooke wounded. The total casualties for the twenty-four hours were one officer killed and one officer and eight other ranks wounded; while, largely as a result of cold and exposure, sixty-four men were admitted to hospital sick before the end of the year. On reaching the horses at Brielen, after a walk through burning Ypres, we found the roads a sheet of ice, and therefore halted till the morning.

This ended the regiment's part in the battle of Ypres, and though the casualties had been considerable, the results more than justified them. For instance, at the canal turn north of Hollebeke, had the enemy forced his way through the regiment, he would have got Klein Zillebeke and Hill 60, and this might well have led to the evacuation of the Ypres Salient and Ypres itself.

The comparatively light casualties were due to the wise leadership of Colonel Howell, and all ranks fully realized that most of us owed our lives to him.

1. Cpl. Wakefield, 4th Hussars, with German prisoner, September 1914. He was killed two days after.
2. Watering in the River Marne near Meaux, September 4th, 1914.
3. "A" Squadron, near Friers, August 28th, 1914. The late Lieut.-Col. J. E. Darley in foreground.   4. Regiment off-saddled near Nouvron, August 30th, 1914.
5. 2nd Troop "A" Squadron, Chauny, August 29th, 1914.
6. On the march, December 1914.

IN THE GREAT WAR

CHAPTER V

21st NOVEMBER, 1914—22nd APRIL, 1915

WINTER QUARTERS, 1914–1915—ZILLEBEKE TRENCHES—LIEUTENANT-COLONEL RANKIN TAKES OVER COMMAND.

WITH the failure of the Germans in the first Battle of Ypres open warfare came to an end for many months—in fact, until the great German attack on the 21st March, 1918. With the exception of several tentative efforts at breaking through, the regiment did no mounted fighting during this period, but was employed in dismounted duty in trenches, in work on back lines of defence, and in training in back billets.

21st Nov., 1914, to 13th Jan., 1915. On the 21st November the regiment marched to various farms near Nooteboom, where it remained in billets to the 13th January. The weather all this time was abominable, while the billets, in the light of future billets, were very inadequate. The majority of the horses were standing out, there were no places for saddlery, and the men were accommodated in dirty farms. Small wonder, then, that lice made their appearance, and some mange amongst the horses, while we continued to have too many cases of sickness. Leave was granted for the first time on the 23rd November for a period of seventy-two hours, confined to officers. This continued at intervals for the rest of the war, but towards the end grew less frequent, and cavalry officers got away only about once in the last year. During this long period in billets most of the time was spent in training, chiefly in dismounted work—*e.g.*, trench mortars and bombing. Inoculation against enteric was also introduced, but was voluntary and unpopular with the men, who required a great deal of " peaceful persuasion " before they would submit to it. Instruction was also given in taking precautions against " trench feet," which was making terrible inroads in the infantry at this time.

On the 2nd December H.M. the King inspected the regiment, and on the 7th December we were inspected by the Field-Marshal Commanding-in-Chief.

14th-31st Jan. On the 14th January we marched to billets in Herbelle and Clety. These were very much better billets, and were sufficiently far from the line to be out of the war atmosphere. The men were getting to know and understand the French better, and altogether the life was more decent and restful. We remained here until the 31st January, training, playing football, and working up the horses, which required a good deal of attention after the hardships they had undergone.

On the 31st January we marched to Outtersteene, and remained in billets there until the 12th February. During this time Captain Davie, R.A.M.C., joined us, and was with us until the 15th March, 1915. He became universally popular, and looked after our wounded on all occasions in the most devoted manner, showing the usual courage of the R.A.M.C. under fire.

1st-12th Feb. At 1.30 on the 12th we left the horses and moved by bus through Ypres to the Ecole de Bienfaisance. Ypres was one degree more destroyed than when we had last seen it, but there were still some shops trading, and most of the buildings were more or less intact. We spent the night there, sending, however, one officer per squadron to spend the night in the trenches with the 10th Hussars, from whom we were to take over. The trenches were adjoining the French on our left and the 4th Cavalry Brigade on our right. They were very wet and muddy, some one to two feet in depth (of mud) for the most part, while there were no luxuries, such as duck-boards.

The parapets were too thin to resist bullets, and the wire was almost non-existent. The only dug-outs were scooped out under the parapet and parados impartially. The line ran through a pinewood, and the broken trees formed a dense abattis between our line and that of the Germans, which ran at a distance of thirty to a hundred yards away. There were a limited number of gumboots, but not nearly enough to go round.

It was necessary to send our own parties nightly for rations and everything else to "Cavan's Dug-out," a distance of two miles through deep and sticky mud, while the wounded had to go nearly as far by stretcher before they could be evacuated. Altogether a cheerless prospect, and one which would have filled with dismay anyone who saw only the finished trench-work of, say, the year 1916, and comparable only to the latter stages of the Somme or Passchendaele battles.

14th Feb. Owing to the late arrival of rations on the 13th February a start was not made until 10 p.m., and it was not until 1 a.m. that we reached the trenches, everyone being by then thoroughly wet to the knees from falling in the dark into shell-holes filled with water. We were not shelled, however, *en route*, but the reliefs were not completed until 3 a.m.

When it grew light the next day we were able to gauge the situation better, and found that it had its compensations—*e.g.*, owing to trenches being so close, we could not be shelled. The French on our left had had considerable experience already of trench warfare, and, being more adaptable as a race, had made themselves much more comfortable.

We, of course, were entirely new to the work, and had everything to learn, and no one to teach us except our neighbours the French. We got on very well with the latter, and bartered rations with them considerably. For instance, for a pot of jam (this was before the plum-and-apple epoch) we got two loaves of French bread, but we did not swap our rum for their *vin rouge*.

THE 4TH (QUEEN'S OWN) HUSSARS

It is worth examining the orders issued by Colonel Howell on the 14th February :—

1. Following reports required daily—
    By 7.30 a.m. : casualty report ; requirements in R.E. material.
    At 5 a.m., 1 p.m., 4 p.m. : report on general situation.

2. Fifty per cent. of all ranks will be on duty by night, 25 per cent. by day. Of the latter, an observer with periscope should be in observation about every twenty yards, and remainder plus extra fatigue parties should be at work in improving defences and drainage.

3. Mackintoshes are to be worn by all ranks on or off duty when out in the rain.

4. Drainage is all important, and must start from the left and be carried down to the stream on the right, and thence into the German lines.

5. Latrines want improvement, and must be marked.

6. Spare articles of equipment—*e.g.*, gum-boots—to be collected and sent to Headquarters.

7. All N.C.Os. down to section leaders must know thoroughly geography of their own squadron trenches and of sectors on left and right of them.

8. In event of alarm, trenches to be manned rapidly and quietly, with the idea of surprising the enemy—to be practised once by day and once by night.

As to 1, these reports seemed sufficiently numerous at the time, but were child's play compared to the reports and returns required a year later in the trenches.

The number on duty in 2 appears very large, but everyone in these early days of trench warfare was at a high tension, and it was difficult to realize that the enemy could be only thirty yards away and yet remain quiescent for perhaps months at a time.

IN THE GREAT WAR

The necessity for order No. 3 emphasizes the happy-go-lucky disposition of the British soldier, who usually prefers to get wet rather than be encumbered with superfluous coverings.

The drainage of these trenches alone absorbed the constant work of almost half the garrison, for the soil was clay, and soon formed a thick cream of a foot in depth, the consistency of which made it difficult to move with a spade or to persuade to move by force of gravity.

The latrines were indeed capable of improvement, and were also so sited as to be under the fire of an enterprising sniper who was fond of showing a misplaced sense of humour of which he was evidently possessed.

No. 6 foreshadowed the coming of the Salvage Corps, but it is to be feared that very little salved material got beyond our regimental Headquarters, owing to lack of transport.

No. 7 was a point to be insisted upon, for in these trenches, with communication only through a sea of mud, we all tended to become very insular.

In all this work we were much helped by the Field Squadron, R.E. It was at this time under the command of Major Johnson, and was later in the war commanded by Major Swinburne, who was killed in the retreat of March, 1918, while still in command. The amount of work this squadron put in was amazing, and the way in which the most perilous tasks were carried out by them was a lesson to us all. Major Swinburne in particular was absolutely fearless, and we all had the greatest admiration for him.

On this first day sniping was only moderately active, but judged by later standards there may be said to have been "unusual activity" even on this day. At night there were constant outbursts of firing, which took some stopping, and which the French did nothing to lessen by their habit of firing section volleys from left to right of their line every quarter of an hour. This was intended to show the enemy they were on the *qui vive*, but had the effect of keeping even those who should have been resting very much on the *qui vive* also. We soon grew to learn, however, that no noise need alarm us until the machine guns began to open, when it was time to sit up and take notice. The French also told us at 8 p.m. that some deserters had just come in, who said the enemy would attack that night or the next day.

The night of the 14th and the morning of the 15th were very noisy owing to sniping and bursts of fire from both sides. On our side we did a good deal of sniping, but the enemy had had the start of us, and seemed to spot our snipers very quickly. They also annoyed us a good deal by blowing in our sandbags by continuous sniping at the same spot, and caused one or two casualties each day. By night, too, they fired heavy stuff into Ypres, and in particular had a 17-inch howitzer, the shell of which made a noise like an express train going over, and burst in the town with a tremendous crash and echoing reverberations.

15th-18th Feb. The 15th to the 18th were similarly passed in working and sniping. Captain Scott amused himself by playing German airs on a tin whistle to the Germans thirty yards away, but the only answer was said to be a gruff " You wait !" from the Boche. On the 17th we heard digging on our left, and as we had heard of one or two mines having been blown in the French sector about Vermelles, we paid particular attention to listening. The night of the 17th was remarkably quiet, the Germans probably effecting a relief. On the 18th the same sounds were heard, and we could see earth being thrown up from the trench opposite our left. Colonel Howell proposed to make a bombing attack on this point, but, by the request of the French, this was not carried out. To cover the sounds of digging, the enemy were continually firing, and bullets were coming over pretty thick.

Meanwhile Lieutenants Hayhurst - France, Sykes, Sowerby, Godson, and Ainslie had joined our led horses.

19th Feb. Our relief arrived at 12.30 a.m. on the 19th ; they were the 16th Lancers, and we marched back to the Ecole de Bienfaisance.

Colonel Howell made some notes on the trenches, in which he pointed out that the trench near the junction with the French was probably mined, and also suggested improvements—*e.g.*, turning the support trench there into a fire trench for use in the event of the front line being blown up. These notes were handed over to the relieving troops.

The relief was complete by 3.20 a.m., when we marched back to the Ecole de Bienfaisance, arriving at 5.15 a.m., and rested all day. We were now in support to the troops in the line, and were confined to billets.

20th Feb. The 20th was also spent here, some desultory shelling in the near vicinity going on all day.

21st Feb. At 6.45 a.m. on the 21st the following message was received from Colonel Greenly, the G.S.O. 1 of the Division :—" Turn your command out at once, but do not move till further orders. Germans have blown up one of our left trenches, and 16th Lancers ordered to counter-attack."

At 7.30 a.m. this further message was received :—" Move your command to Cavan's House at once, informing me by bearer when it starts."

At 9.15 Colonel Howell sent the following message to General Chetwode, commanding 5th Cavalry Brigade :—" Head of 4th Hussars just arrived here at French village (a hut camp behind Cavan's House). One company French infantry now marching off to support 16th Lancers. What is situation, and what orders for me ?"

Colonel Howell then went to Cavan's House and got on the 'phone to General Chetwode. From him he learnt that a squadron of 20th Hussars and some French had already counter-attacked, but had failed to reach the captured trench. He was further ordered to counter-attack immediately on arrival on the scene of action, but the telephone broke down at this moment, Colonel Howell remarking : " A deaf ear at the telephone may be as useful as a blind eye at a telescope."

THE 4TH (QUEEN'S OWN) HUSSARS

The regiment moved then to the trenches we had occupied before, and remained in close support behind them. There we found that the Germans had blown a mine just where we had suspected its presence, the 16th losing heavily in officers—seven killed and four wounded.

The squadron of the 20th and some French were lying out just behind the trench, the Germans in occupation and keeping up a heavy fire, which prevented our men from advancing or retiring. Colonel Howell was put in charge of the sector, and given a squadron of 5th Lancers in addition, and a total of twelve machine guns. It was then decided not to counter-attack again, but to dig a trench across the rear of the one lost, thus cutting off our former salient there. Then to make it as unpleasant as possible for the Germans there by the use of our one trench mortar, bombs, and rifle and machine-gun fire.

This was done, we putting one squadron into the line, the remainder in support and digging.

The remainder of the day was very noisy, but casualties were few, we having three men wounded, Captain Stokes, returning from leave, being hit before he reached us, and, as it turned out, being incapacitated for the rest of the war.

We remained in the same positions all night, while bombing and firing went on and work was continued on the new trench and dug-outs. The next day passed in a similar manner,

22nd Feb. and at nightfall the 4th Hussars were withdrawn to Ypres, and moved off at 9.30 to busses west of Ypres.

23rd-25th Feb. We arrived at our horses at 6.30 a.m. on the 23rd, after sliding at intervals off the roads. The 24th and 25th February were spent in billets there.

26th Feb. to 9th Mar. At 7.15 a.m. we marched to Herbelle, arriving at our former billets at 1.15 p.m., where we remained until March 9th, carrying out training chiefly on the lessons learnt during our tour in the trenches.

Major A. D. Bell joined on the 2nd March, while Captain

IN THE GREAT WAR

Gannon left for hospital on the 6th March. On the 9th March the regiment marched at 6.45 a.m. via Ebblinghem and Hazebrouck to inadequate billets at Le Parc. Orders were received to be ready to march any time after 9 a.m. the next day at one hour's notice.

10th Mar. On the 10th we concentrated at La Motte at 4.30 p.m., but were at once sent back, being told we should probably move at 7 a.m. the next day to La Couronne.

11th Mar. At 5.30 a.m. on the 11th we marched to La Couronne, remained there until the evening, and then went into billets between Neuf Berquin and Doulieu, in readiness to move at one hour's notice after 8.30 a.m. the next day.

12th Mar. On the 12th March we remained in billets until 5 p.m., when the Brigade concentrated at Neuf Berquin, remaining there until 7.30 p.m., when we returned to billets, receiving orders to concentrate at same place at 7 a.m. the next day; but at 9.30 p.m. orders were received to remain in billets the next day, standing to from 7 a.m. onwards.

13th Mar. On the 13th March, at 3.45 p.m., the regiment marched back to the former billets at Le Parc, where we found Lieutenant Austin with a small reinforcement.

The movements of these last few days were in accordance with the fortunes of the Battle of Neuve Chapelle, then going on to our front, and indicate the fluctuating situation.

14th Mar. On the 14th March Lieutenant-Colonel Howell left the regiment, becoming B.G.G.S. to the Cavalry Corps.

He had been in command of the regiment since the 1st September, 1914, and by his skilful leading had time and again saved the regiment many casualties. His departure was a great loss, but his talents would have been wasted as a regimental commander. He was subsequently killed when carrying out a reconnaissance near Pozières in the latter stages of the Somme Battle of 1916, when acting as B.G.G.S. of the 2nd Corps; his death, it is not too much to say, being a heavy loss to the Army.

THE 4TH (QUEEN'S OWN) HUSSARS

He was succeeded in command by Major Rankin, of the 7th Hussars, who had been attached to the 9th Lancers as a squadron leader during the war. Though a stranger to the regiment, he soon became universally popular, and proved an ideal Commanding Officer in billets and in the field.

Captain Scott left the regiment here to go to the R.F.C., as did Lieutenant Heyman. Second-Lieutenant Godson went to the Base.

13th Mar. to 22nd April From the 13th March to the 22nd April the regiment remained in billets at Le Parc, during which time training was carried on and pack transport was to a large extent substituted for wheels—*e.g.*, for machine guns, tools, and ammunition. Lieutenant Fleetwood Wilson was given the command of machine guns in place of Captain King, who went to England on the 12th March.

IN THE GREAT WAR

CHAPTER VI

23RD APRIL—30TH MAY, 1915

FIRST GERMAN GAS ATTACK—WIELTJE—HOOGE

23rd April AT 9.30 a.m. on the 23rd April news was received of the first German gas attack, and at 12 noon the brigade concentrated at Vieux Berquin and marched north via the Mont des Cats to a point two miles south-south-east of Poperinghe, where we bivouacked at 10.30 p.m. During the day a good many French colonial troops were encountered, scattered about, and all night very heavy fire was heard to the north. The general impression was that things were very critical, and that if the Germans had a large force available to follow up their initial gas success, they would probably break right through. From the light of after knowledge this impression seems to have been a correct one, and to this day it is difficult for the regimental officer to understand why the Germans made such a feeble effort to push home their success.

24th April At 4 a.m. on the 24th orders were received to concentrate immediately at the cross-roads south of R in Reninghelst. Thence we marched to concentrate south-south-west of Elverdinghe. There the horses were left, and at 9.30 a.m. we advanced dismounted to the west bank of the canal, one and a half miles north of Ypres. During this march a good many shells fell near and amongst the column, but no one was hit. Here we remained in position, in support of the Canadians, until 2 p.m., while French troops went forward on their right to attack, but, as far as could be ascertained, they reached only the same alignment as the Canadians. The latter were full of fight and very pleased with themselves, as they might well be, for they had thus, the first time they were seriously engaged, held up a further enemy advance in what might have proved a very dangerous situation.

At 2 p.m. we returned to the horses near Elverdinghe and bivouacked, with orders to be ready to turn out at 5 a.m. the next day. During the day some shells had dropped near the horses, and German aeroplanes had dropped some bombs, but without doing any damage.

25th April On the 25th April we remained here until 10 p.m., and then marched circuitously to the huts near Vlamertinghe, dropping the horses *en route*.

26th April On April the 26th, at 5 p.m., we moved off to the G.H.Q. reserve line, near Hell Fire Corner, the level-crossing outside Ypres on the Menin road. We marched dismounted, leading pack-horses. The route was via the western edge of Ypres, and then along the railway line. There was no shelling until the line was reached, but on approaching the railway cutting shells began to fall, but luckily they were nearly all short to our right. Still, it was an unpleasant march, and great difficulty was experienced in keeping the pack-ponies up with the column. On arriving at Hell Fire Corner we filed into the trenches north of it, and found them shallow, badly traversed, and partly enfiladed by guns firing apparently from the direction of Klein Zillebeke.

We got settled in by 11 p.m., having had five men wounded, and spent the night in improving the trenches.

Here the regiment remained for the next three days, the Headquarters being in a farm near the Menin road. This received a good deal of attention, and was finally destroyed a week or two **27th April** later. On the 27th our "A" Echelon, bringing rations through Ypres, was shelled in the town, and had eight horses killed and three men wounded. A sergeant was wounded in the trenches.

IN THE GREAT WAR

At 8.30 p.m. a digging party of five officers and 100 men was sent to Hooge, and worked on the trenches there all night from Hooge to Wieltje. There was desultory shelling all day. Colonel Rankin, who had been on leave, rejoined here.

28th April The 28th was spent in these trenches, three officers and fifty men going to Hooge at night; one man was killed and one wounded.

29th April We remained in trenches on the 29th April until 10 p.m., and then marched to Wieltje to relieve part of the Northumbrian Territorial Division. This division had had a very bad time at St. Julien during the fighting there the previous few days, and had lost so heavily that they no longer had the fine fighting efficiency they had started with from England only ten days before.

We found them in a field lying in shallow scrapes in the ground, and spent a very busy night in deepening these and providing overhead cover against aeroplane observation. Roofing materials appeared from nowhere as by magic, and by daylight not a man was showing above ground. We had learnt at least some of the lessons of the war.

30th April to 2nd May Much time, too, was spent in getting into touch with local commanders in the front line and in support, and altogether no one got very much sleep that night. The next two days were spent in the same field, while at night we built a series of strong posts behind the G.H.Q. line for machine guns to occupy in case of attack.

The line here was somewhat peculiar, as just north of Wieltje the support line joined up with the front line, while east and south of the village the front line ran away out towards the German line. We were just behind the support line beside Wieltje village. A sergeant and one man were wounded during the two days.

2nd May On the 2nd May the day was quite quiet until 5.30 p.m., when shelling began to our front. On looking out from our shelters we saw a greenish-yellow cloud, about

THE 4TH (QUEEN'S OWN) HUSSARS

20 feet high by half a mile broad, sweeping down from the northeast with a favouring breeze from St. Julien. It should be noted here that we had as yet no gas masks, and our only protection against gas was 4-inch by 2-inch of flannelette, which we were told to dampen and hold over the nose and mouth.

The machine-gun detachment was immediately sent up to occupy one of the redoubts dug the night before east of Wieltje, and they got there about the same time as the gas.

Infantry now began pouring back, suffering to a greater or less degree from gas poisoning (some of them died that evening in our shelters). They were a very dreadful sight, and those not yet helpless were nevertheless oblivious to everything except the gas cloud which was following and enveloping them. The regiment was now ordered forward, and, led by Colonel Rankin, advanced at the double through the gas and a heavy howitzer barrage to take the place of the infantry who had come back. It looked, of course, as though the front line had gone, and advancing German infantry were expected to come into view at any moment following up their gas cloud. On reaching the support line, however, on the left of the Carabiniers, it was found that the infantry had come from this trench, and the regiment went into it. Still, it was not clear whether the front line was held until Sergeant Siddons, after a fine reconnaissance of the front line under heavy shell fire, brought back the information that the front line still held. We then remained in the support line.

The casualties were one man killed, two officers and twenty-two other ranks wounded. We thus got off very lightly, the proportion of wounded to killed being remarkably high. Everyone felt somewhat weak after inhaling the gas, but no one suffered any serious after-effects, probably because we went straight through it and into the pure air beyond.

(*See* Appendix E for a report on the conduct of the 4th Hussars on this occasion.)

IN THE GREAT WAR

3rd May — At 1 a.m. on the 3rd May, much to everyone's surprise, we were relieved, and marched on foot to Ouderdom, past the Zillebeke dam. As we reached this point it began to grow light, and a tremendous din broke out to our left, while the green cloud was seen in the distance above the trees. It was the Germans delivering their final successful assault on Hill 60. No one who was there is likely to forget that march through the meadows and orchards of Ypres on that wonderful May morning, with the apple-trees all in bloom and nature at its most beautiful, while behind us was the horrid din of war, with that foul green cloud hanging over the forest.

The horses were picked up at Ouderdom and the march resumed to Wormhoudt, where we billeted, spending the next two days in cleaning up and resting.

6th May — At 1 p.m. on the 6th May we marched via Cassel and Caestre to billets in La Rue du Bois, where we remained on short notice to the 13th May.

13th May — At 11.30 p.m. on that date a very terse message was received. It read: "Embus at once for Ypres."

It turned out later that the 3rd Cavalry Division had been heavily attacked, and, in spite of a fine counter-attack, the line had been driven in.

14th-22nd May — At 2 a.m. the busses arrived, and 14 officers and 296 other ranks moved to the Vlamertinghe Huts. At 7.30 p.m. on the 14th we marched via Ypres, which was being shelled and was littered with dead men and horses, to support the 5th Cavalry Brigade, who were in the front line about Verlorenhoek. We were in the G.H.Q. line in front of Potijze. We remained here until the 22nd, having a fairly quiet time on the whole. One man killed and two wounded. Our "A" Echelon perhaps had the worst time bringing rations nightly to the Potijze cross-roads, and being shelled *en route*.

22nd May — At midnight on the 22nd we were relieved and marched to Vlamertinghe, where we remained the next day also.

THE 4TH (QUEEN'S OWN) HUSSARS

24th May At 3 a.m. on the 24th May we were awakened by the coughing and spitting of partially gassed men coming through the village after being gassed out of the trenches at Hooge and the Bellewaarde Ridge.

At 4.30 a.m. we concentrated at the T-roads south-east of Vlamertinghe, while the enemy shelled the Ypres road with lachrymatory shells, very irritable to the eyes, nose and throat. Though annoying and having at first some moral effect, owing to our ignorance of them, these shells did less real damage than ordinary high explosive would have done. At 10.30 a.m. the regiment marched across country through Ypres, which was being fairly heavily shelled, to our old friend the Ecole de Bienfaisance (somewhat ironically named under the present circumstances). From here we moved to the railway cutting south-east of Ypres, which we found full of troops. We put one squadron here, and the others and the machine guns remained in the open in its vicinity. The cutting was very heavily shelled, chiefly with lachrymatory shells, and it proved rather a death-trap. There was a remarkable *melange* of troops of many units there. Here S.S.M. Hawgood, who had distinguished himself throughout the war by his bravery, was killed, while twelve men were wounded—once more a very fortunate proportion of wounded to killed.

An infantry brigade passed through us during the afternoon, going up to attack the Bellewaarde Ridge. They were spotted as they passed us, and were received with heavy and well-directed shell fire, and their advance was stopped before reaching the objective. Altogether a very unpleasant afternoon.

At dark the shelling pretty well ceased, and the regiment moved up to relieve troops holding Hooge. There we found very great confusion of units, all very dazed from the effects of the gas. The regiment took over from the 9th Lancers and Territorial Buffs and Durham Light Infantry, retaining forty men of the Buffs and ninety of the Durhams.

IN THE GREAT WAR

25th May As soon as it grew light on the 25th we were able to get some grasp of the situation. The position seemed to be as follows:—Enemy holding Bellewaarde Ridge strongly, with trenches facing west and north on the west end of the ridge and in the small wood on the end of the spur, with communication trenches running back past Bellewaarde Farm. Apparently there were no fire trenches on the southern slopes of the ridge, but between Bellewaarde Pond and Hooge Chateau were two small trenches. It was not until the morning of the 26th, when we got a map off a German officer killed on the road, that we got a clear idea of the German defences.

There was a hostile machine-gun post on the northern bank of the Menin road, some 100 yards from our own road post. On our east front were snipers' trenches from 50 to 300 yards away, with their main trenches (judging from rifle fire at our aeroplanes) 500 to 600 yards distant. Most of the village north of the road was therefore a No Man's Land, with many corpses, British and German, in the buildings, gardens, and tangled undergrowth. On our immediate left there was a gap of 1,000 yards down the Menin road to the Birr cross-roads, which was held by our infantry. The Germans showed no inclination to push through here, and they may not have been aware that the gap existed.

Our right, 250 yards from the road, ended at Sanctuary Wood, and after a short gap the 5th Lancers held the line. Our right trenches were full of springs, which were continually causing the sides to fall in, exposing our men—a circumstance of which the German snipers were not slow in availing themselves.

On our left, under the western house of Hooge, was a vast dugout, constructed by the French early in the year as a *poste de commandement*. The interior of this was a grisly sight, for a shell had come through, killing several men, and in addition there were gassed and wounded men there of the fighting of the day before. In the house across the road, in a room on the first storey, was a gigantic German corpse. We called it the House of the Green Man.

How he came there was a mystery. There was some sniping and shelling during the 25th.

26th May At dawn on the 26th, when it was still a little misty, a German officer and N.C.O. walked up to our barricade on the road. On being summoned to surrender, the officer appeared to attempt to draw his pistol, and they were both shot dead. On the N.C.O. were many interesting papers, including a pocket-book containing what appeared to be code names for various munition works in the United States. This man had been in Europe only about a fortnight, and was wearing an Iron Cross, so he appeared to have been a spy of some standing.

The night before the R.Es. had put out a belt of concertina wire between the road and the chateau stables, and during the day we constructed some strong points behind the wire north of the road.

As soon as it was clear enough the enemy sent up an aeroplane a short distance in front of us, which flew to and fro, low and a very short distance away, apparently photographing. We had so little reserve small-arms ammunition that we could not afford to shoot at him much, and failed to drive him away.

There was some sniping and shelling by the enemy all day. We, on our part, had some very pretty sniping at Germans on the Bellewaarde Ridge; the range was 900 yards, but a good many hits were recorded. Our guns were entirely inactive, for this was the period when the shell shortage was at its most acute stage. During this and subsequent nights patrols were sent out as far as the chateau stables, but though hostile patrols were heard, no encounter actually took place. At nightfall the Buffs and Durham Light Infantry were withdrawn, being relieved by a company of the East Yorks (Territorial), but the latter were kept back in support at Zouave Wood, only coming up at night to dig.

27th May On the 27th May we were harassed by sniping and by a *minenwerfer*, which did some damage on our left trenches. The only shelling from our own guns was unfortunately directed on our own trenches, and we had the greatest difficulty in stopping this. Eventually a gunner observer was got up, and it transpired then that they had thought our trenches were occupied by the enemy, and they had refrained from shooting at the Bellewaarde Ridge, believing it to be held by our troops !

We got more machine guns this day, which were disposed as follows :—Two guns in right advanced post on the Menin road (20th Hussars); two guns in left advanced post on the west end of Hooge (12th Lancers); two guns to the left rear of the latter, commanding the hill west of Hooge on the Menin road (Oxford Yeomanry). The gap between our left and the Birr cross-roads was filled this night and subsequent nights by posts of the Gordons, with whom we kept touch.

28th May On the 28th the *minenwerfer* was busy in the morning, but after that things quieted down. During the morning a man, fairly severely gassed and very incoherent, came into our lines from north of the road. He stated he had been lying out in No Man's Land for some days, but did not know how long, nor could he describe exactly where he had been. He had a message signed by an officer, Sayer by name, which stated that the officer was still lying out with a broken leg, unable to move. He endeavoured to explain his position, but it was very vague, and the man who brought it in was so confused owing to his gassing that his description of the place was not worth much. Several parties went out to search on this and subsequent days, but found nothing but a revolver belt. Some time afterwards a Lieutenant Sayer was reported a prisoner-of-war, so presumably he was found by a German patrol and removed.

At night the Germans carried out a relief, some of their troops apparently getting very drunk in celebrating it. One party came up to our left advanced post through the bushes, shouting out, " God punish England !" Bombs were thrown at them, hitting at least one, and they made off with cries of pain. There was a great deal of sniping going on also.

THE 4TH (QUEEN'S OWN) HUSSARS

29th May At 9.30 a.m. on the 29th a party of fifty Germans, carrying tools, in two parties, entered the chateau stables from the south-west corner of the lake, passing 200 yards in front of our left post. We allowed them to enter, but trained machine guns on the approaches to the stables, and asked for a gun to open fire on the building. This took a long time to get, as, owing again to the shortage of ammunition, it was necessary for the heavy guns to get special permission from the corps before they were allowed to fire a round. Meanwhile an officer and six men approached our left post, when four of them were killed. An hour later twelve ran for it out of the stables towards their own lines; six were killed by the machine guns. At last a 4·5 howitzer opened fire, and after two direct hits the whole party of Germans bolted, and were caught by our cross machine-gun fire, which knocked out twenty of them—a very successful little affair. The rest of the day was quiet. At 9.30 p.m. a German officer's patrol entered the chateau, and came out at midnight.

Our orders all this time were to remain strictly on the defensive. At first the orders, in event of a serious attack, were to retire to Sanctuary Wood. This was afterwards changed, and we were ordered to hold on at all costs.

Half an hour after midnight the regiment was relieved by the 3rd Dragoon Guards.

This tour in the trenches cost us rather heavy casualties considering there was no attack: they were five killed, twenty-eight wounded, and twelve sick, the latter due to the wet in the trenches on our right. Nevertheless we had the satisfaction of knowing that we had inflicted heavier losses than we had incurred.

30th May In the morning of the 30th we marched to Vlamertinghe, and thence went by bus to La Rue du Bois. Everyone was about " all in " by this time, and a rest was very welcome.

IN THE GREAT WAR

CHAPTER VII

31st MAY, 1915—15th MARCH, 1917

THE SUMMER OF 1915 — BATTLE OF LOOS—WINTER QUARTERS, 1915–16 — VERMELLES TRENCHES — SOMME BATTLE, 1916 — WINTER QUARTERS, 1916–17.

31st May to 15th July
ON the 31st May we moved to fresh billets near Staple, where we remained until the 15th July. During this time Major Mockett rejoined from England, and Lieutenants Alcock, Buddicom, and Close joined. At the end of this period Captain Scott rejoined. Training was carried out all the time, and on the 1st July three officers and 200 men were sent up to construct trenches in the neighbourhood of Dickebusch. This party was relieved in batches at intervals, and was withdrawn on the 4th September. Casualties were very few—one man killed and three wounded.

16th July to 20th Sept.
On the 16th July billets were moved to Wulverdinghe, and again on the 5th August to Blessy and Marthes, where we remained until the 20th September; but the training became of a more mobile nature, based on a theoretical " break through " of the enemy's lines.

21st Sept.
On the 21st September the regiment moved to Flechin, " A " Echelon being brigaded and " B " Echelon left at Roquetoire.

24th Sept.
On the 24th September we marched to Bermicourt.

25th Sept.
On the 25th September the regiment stood-to from " Réveillé " at forty minutes' notice. At 3.15 p.m. orders were received to concentrate at once at Trois

THE 4TH (QUEEN'S OWN) HUSSARS

Vaux. From here we marched to Marles les Mines through heavy traffic, and bivouacked there, hearing *en route* various exaggerated stories of the Battle of Loos. The next few days were spent standing-to at various notice, and can be described shortly.

26th Sept. Standing-to at forty minutes' notice.

27th Sept. At 3.40 a.m. orders received to saddle up ready to march at 5 a.m. At 4.50 a.m. orders cancelled; forty minutes' stand-to again in force.

28th Sept. At 12.20 a.m. ordered to be ready to march at 5.30 a.m. At 5.30 a.m. orders cancelled; stand-to at one and a half hour's notice. At 8 p.m. stand-to at three hours' notice.

29th Sept. to 14th Oct. On the 29th September, at 8.15 a.m., moved to new cramped billets at Bellery, where we remained until the 14th October. On the 1st October a party of 100 men proceeded by bus to Vermelles, and were employed in burying the dead and digging trenches. One man was wounded, and they rejoined on the 4th.

14th Oct. to 20th Oct. On the 14th October we moved to new billets at Ligny, and stayed there to the 20th October, and then returned to the old billets at Blessy, etc.

21st Oct. to 17th Nov. On the 21st October Lieutenants Delius and Fisher-Smith joined with 100 dismounted men, extra to establishment. Lieutenant Arkwright and Captain Rotheram also joined, but the former went to hospital on the 26th.

On October the 30th a digging party of three officers and 100 men went to Ebblinghem to work on a reserve line, being increased to 200 on the 5th November. Captain Mewburn, of the 14th Hussars, left to rejoin his own regiment on this date, and was subsequently killed with them in Mesopotamia. Major Darley was sent to England on the 11th November to take over an infantry battalion. When he got there he found no battalion ready for him, and after five months he was sent back again.

IN THE GREAT WAR

17th Nov. On the 17th November we moved in a snowstorm to Vaudringhem, and here the horses remained until the 19th June, while we found various trench parties and working parties, and also carried on steady training, chiefly dismounted up to March, but after that chiefly mounted, doing training with the brigade and then the division.

During December the digging party was at Renescure until the 29th, when it returned to billets.

1st Jan., 1916. On the 1st January, 1916, eight officers and 300 men went into trenches at Vermelles. They formed one company, the 5th and 16th Lancers forming the other two, and the whole was known as the 3rd Dismounted Battalion, each cavalry regiment in turn finding the Headquarters. The 4th Hussars found the Headquarters from the 25th January to the 15th February. During all this time the horses had only one man to five horses, and they naturally fell away in condition very considerably.

This was the first time that the regiment experienced trench warfare on scientific lines. Our former tours in the line had been before the system had been properly organized, and the trenches had consisted of one line only with a few off-shoots. At Vermelles all was entirely different. There were many lines of trenches resulting from the many actions fought there. At the end of 1914 the French had taken Vermelles, blowing the first large mine of the war under the chateau there; they had taken several lines of trenches there. In the murderous Battle of Loos, in September, 1915, the British had further advanced up to the Quarries, with the famous Hohenzollern Redoubt on the left, and the whole overlooked by the big dump of Fosse 8, which itself had been held for a few hours during the battle by a Kitchener brigade. The sector held by the dismounted 2nd Cavalry Division ran from the Vermelles—Hulluch road on the right across the front of the Quarries to the beginning of the Hohenzollern Redoubt on the left.

THE 4TH (QUEEN'S OWN) HUSSARS

The whole front line was more or less honeycombed with mines run out by either side, and existence in the front trenches was somewhat precarious. Both sides also possessed numbers of spring bomb-throwers, rifle grenades, and trench mortars.

There was a very thorough telephone system throughout these trenches, which greatly facilitated communication. There were two objections to telephones, however—firstly, they were always cut by a bombardment; and, secondly, conversations over them could be overhead by the enemy with the help of some apparatus, and any secret communications were therefore sent by runner. For this purpose a number of men were trained as trench runners, and very well did they carry out their duties.

Our signallers also were continually mending breaks in the lines under shell fire.

Communication trenches ran all the way from the front trench to the village of Vermelles.

The trenches were in fair order only when we took over, and the enemy snipers were very troublesome; but after a week or two the whole trench system was wonderfully well drained and built up, and the enemy snipers entirely got under by unremitting counter-sniping.

The system of relief was by dismounted brigades, which did three days in the front line, three in support, and three in reserve.

Of the support battalion, one company was in Curly Crescent, one in Vermelles (in the mine-shaft), and one in Noyelles.

A composite party of bombers was organized from the brigade, and machine guns and trench mortars were similarly pooled and run independently of the battalion. Their relief was arranged to take place on different dates to that of the battalion, thus ensuring that some of the garrison always remained in the line while the remainder was being relieved.

It is not intended to give a detailed diary of events during all this tour in the trenches, as one day was much the same as another. The salient events only will be described.

IN THE GREAT WAR

The first striking difference in these trenches to the former ones was the surprising number of reports and returns asked for. The following were the regular standing reports and returns rendered by battalions; in addition were very many others.

1. By 4.30 a.m. and 4.30 p.m.: Morning and evening wire. To contain all important information on the situation, and some account of shelling on both sides in the front line.

2. Progress report by 3 p.m. Work done in front line.

3. Battle casualties by 11 a.m.; ordinary casualties by 10.30 a.m.

4. Duplicate receipt for all trench stores taken or handed over.

5. Certificate once a week that smoke helmets had been inspected and all deficiencies made good.

6. Certificate that each man had a spare pair of socks.

7. Return of reinforcements required and received (each Thursday).

8. Fighting strength return daily.

9. Tactical progress report by 4 p.m. daily, comprising—
   - (*a*) Work carried out on our line.
   - (*b*) Operations, our own and enemy: shelling, sniping, trench mortar, etc.
   - (*c*) Information. Everything new noticed during the twenty-four hours in enemy lines—*e.g.*, machine guns located, hostile movements, work on trenches or on wire, etc.

All the above were in addition to the returns required from regiments in the ordinary way. We had in the trenches auxiliary troops—R.Es., miners, and observers for heavy and field guns. Constant and close liaison was required with these. The mining and counter-mining was carried on with extreme secrecy, and we knew little of this branch of warfare except when warned by our miners to vacate a portion of trench or to supply fatigues to carry away earth from one of our own shafts. On the whole, this mining, though it had some moral effect, was more of a nuisance to both sides than a source of casualties.

4th-5th Jan. The 4th and 5th January were spent in the front line. Nothing worthy of note occurred, but enemy sniping was very severe.

6th-9th Jan. The 6th to 9th were spent in support in Vermelles and Noyelles, but strong working parties were furnished for the front system.

10th-12th Jan. The 10th, 11th and 12th were spent in the trenches, and much work was done during the period.

13th-18th Jan. The 13th to 18th were spent in Noyelles in reserve, but working parties of about 150 per regiment were always out.

19th-21st Jan. The 19th to 21st were spent in front line; a fairly quiet time, as by now the enemy snipers had been got under.

22nd-26th Jan. The 22nd to 26th were spent in Vermelles, etc., as support battalion; 4th Hussars Headquarters took over the battalion.

26th Jan. At 6.30 p.m. on the 26th we were ordered to stand-to, as an attack was expected, commencing with an artillery bombardment at 8 p.m.

This alarm was probably caused by the fact that the 27th was the Kaiser's birthday, and therefore some sort of frightfulness on the part of the Germans was to be expected.

At 7 p.m. the supports moved up, the 4th Hussars going to O.B.1, the Headquarters to Curly Crescent, the various trenches being thus filled with troops. However, no attack took place, and the night was quiet.

27th-28th Jan. During the night 27th–28th we moved up to the front line, the 4th Hussars going into the left sector of the front trench. Work was carried on all day, while the enemy shelled all the trenches lightly. At 7.15 p.m. the enemy blew a small mine on our right, and we stood-to for half an hour till all was quiet again.

IN THE GREAT WAR

29th Jan. It was quiet up to dawn on the 29th, when the Germans were seen to test the wind by putting up smoke. At 10.30 a.m. Lieutenant Wass reported that German bombers had sapped up to our line and were bombing; one of their bombs fell on a steel helmet (which were issued here for the first time) and glanced off, doing no harm. This was the first of many lives saved by steel helmets in the regiment.

From 12 to 2 p.m. our front line was trench-mortared, great damage being done to the trenches. It started again later and did more damage. At 3.45 p.m., the site of the mortar or mortars having been fairly accurately located, a 4·5 battery fired forty rounds and silenced the enemy fire. At nightfall Sergeant Siddons and Private Shaw went out and reconnoitred thoroughly the front of our line, especially the reported sap. They found the latter was only a disused trench. For this reconnaissance both received decorations.

30th Jan. The 30th was a very foggy day, and was therefore very quiet. It was possible to walk about on top just behind the front line, and many grisly relics of the Loos battle were found.

31st Jan. to 5th Feb. The 31st Jan. to the 5th Feb. were spent in Noyelles in reserve, finding working parties. A German aeroplane dropped a bomb, but beyond breaking up two huts this did no damage.

6th Feb. On the early morning of the 6th February we relieved 5th Battalion in the front line. At 4.10 a.m. the Germans exploded a large mine just in front of the 16th Lancers' trenches. It was preceded and followed by heavy rifle grenade and mortar fire all along our front. Our artillery barrage, got on by 'phone, was prompt and effective, and the 16th succeeded in occupying the crater.

The O.C. troops in this sector, Lieutenant-Colonel Rankin, received the congratulations of the Commander-in-Chief on the arrangements made against this mine.

THE 4TH (QUEEN'S OWN) HUSSARS

6th-8th Feb. For the remainder of this tour in the front trenches, up to the night of the 8th, the enemy were very busy with mortars and rifle grenades, chiefly on the 4th Hussars' sector, and we had a good many casualties.

9th-13th Feb. The 9th to the 13th was spent in support, 4th Hussars being in Noyelles. At 11.30 p.m. on the 13th the enemy blew several mines on our front, and the support was moved up. Lieutenant Trew, who was in charge of the battalion bombers, went up and did very good work there all night. He was recommended for the Military Cross, but did not get it until a year or two later, on another recommendation, as happened to many recommendations for awards.

14th Feb. On the 14th the battalion was relieved, marched to Sailly la Bourse, billeted there, and the dismounted 4th Hussars returned by train to the Vaudringhem area on the 15th.

During this tour we had seven other ranks killed and thirty-one wounded. There were no casualties to officers.

Captain Radclyffe and Lieutenants Crerar-Gilbert, Coghlan, O'Kelly, and Johnson joined from England.

On the 10th March the machine guns of the brigade were brigaded under Lieutenant Fleetwood Wilson, 4th Hussars, and were called the 3rd Machine Gun Squadron. Hotchkiss guns were also issued, and instruction in their use was given by Captain King.

15th Feb. to 19th June From the 15th February to the 19th June the regiment remained in billets at Vaudringhem. During this time different working parties were furnished to the Second Army. Lieutenant-Colonel Rankin, D.S.O., left the regiment on the 16th April to take over command of an infantry brigade. During the comparatively short time he had been associated with the regiment he had identified himself to a remarkable extent with the 4th Hussars. He was, perhaps, the most popular officer who served with the regiment

Photo by] [Barnett, London

BRIGADIER-GENERAL CHARLES RANKIN, C.M.G., D.S.O.,
who commanded the 4th Hussars from March 1915 to April 16th, 1916.

IN THE GREAT WAR

during the war, and there is no one who served under him who does not remember him with affection.

On the 3rd May Lieutenant-Colonel Darley came out from England and took over command of the regiment.

On the 7th June a dismounted party went up to the Canadian Corps, which was having heavy fighting around St. Eloi. They were used in reserve, and had one man killed. They returned on the 17th June.

19th June to 15th July
On the 19th June the regiment marched by night to La Rue du Bois, where it remained until the 15th July, ready for dismounted service.

15th July to 5th Sept.
On the 15th July the Regiment moved to Strazeele, and remained there until the 5th September, a working party of 300 being furnished to the Second Army until the 2nd September. On the 5th September a dismounted squadron was sent to Albert, and was there employed in making various cavalry tracks up to the front line over the Somme battlefield.

6th Sept.
On the 6th September the regiment marched to L'Ecleme, and thence, via Bours, Qœux, Outrebois, Haravesnes and Bonnay, to near Bray.

13th Sept.
On the 13th September squadron leaders went up to the front line at Longueval to reconnoitre the country over which it was hoped we might operate.

14th Sept.
On the 14th the orders for the attack on the 15th were issued.

15th Sept.
At 10 a.m. on the 15th the regiment stood-to at a quarter of an hour's notice until 6 p.m., but by then it was tolerably clear there would be no break through.

16th Sept.
On the 16th stood-to at four hours' notice.

18th Sept.
On the 18th our working parties on the cavalry tracks were relieved. On the 22nd "B" Squadron was the mounted "duty" squadron at Carnoy, but was not employed. We remained here standing-to at intervals and

finding working parties until the 1st October. Our working parties had three men wounded during this time.

In this camp at Bray the regiment had its first experience of night bombing, a hostile aeroplane dropping a few small bombs without doing damage. It was not until 1918 that night bombing became dangerous, but in that year we suffered considerably from it.

1st Oct. to 8th Nov. On the 1st October we moved bivouac to Meaulte, and remained there until the 8th November. We lived for this period in tents in a sea of mud. The weather was vile, and it was the most uncomfortable and boring period of the whole war. A working party of 120 men and 24 pack-horses were furnished to the 14th and 15th Corps for taking up rations and making roads, etc., for the infantry.

8th Nov. On the 8th November, leaving the pack-horses behind, the regiment marched via Bussy—Bourdon—Hautvillers to Raye, Mouriez, Capelle, and Guinchy to winter billets.

The pack party returned on the 29th.

The billets were good, and temporary stabling was erected where required.

9th Jan. 1917. On the 9th January, 1917, a pioneer company of 8 officers and 246 other ranks went up to Le Brebis to construct new railways, where they remained until the 15th March. During this time partial reliefs were carried out but, owing to shortage of men, the party left with the horses in billets could carry out very little training, which was confined to Hotchkiss gun training, staff rides, and innumerable courses.

15th Mar. On the 15th March the pioneer company rejoined, and on the 25th 2nd-Lieutenant Bell took up a small party of thirteen men per regiment to work on a cavalry track at Arras.

IN THE GREAT WAR

CHAPTER VIII

5TH APRIL, 1917—20TH MARCH, 1918

BATTLE OF ARRAS TO THE BEGINNING OF THE GERMAN OFFENSIVE IN MARCH, 1918

5th April On the 5th April we marched to Hem. On the 7th we marched to Gaudiempre. Here "A" Echelon was brigaded, and "B" Echelon left behind at Occoches.
It should be mentioned here that all the winter, which was an exceptionally severe one, horses had been on 9 lb. of oats per day. Although this was helped out by local purchases of hay, etc., the horses were by the spring in a weak state, and not fit for hard work.

9th April At 8.30 a.m. on the 9th April—this being the opening day of the Arras attack—we marched in a heavy snowstorm to the Arras end of the cavalry track. At 2.30 p.m. we proceeded up this, and formed up between Tilloy and Telegraph Hill. "C" Squadron went on in advance of the brigade to clear a track through Tilloy. The regiment remained on the battlefield at Telegraph Hill until 7 p.m. During the day a wonderful view of the infantry attack was obtained, and we could see our tanks attacking a strong German redoubt at Feuchy Chapelle and clearing it. These views were obtained only in the intervals between heavy snow showers.

At 7 p.m. the regiment returned down the cavalry track, reaching Angy about 2.30 a.m. in heavy snow through very congested traffic. There we bivouacked in the open in the midst of the snow, with a cutting wind blowing. The horses had not been watered from 10.30 a.m. on the 9th to 7 a.m. on the 10th, and had only a little hay on the 10th—none on the 9th.

THE 4TH (QUEEN'S OWN) HUSSARS

10th April At 10 a.m. on the 10th we were ordered to stand-to at half an hour's notice, and at 1.30 p.m. were ordered to turn out.

By 2 p.m. we were *en route*, and reached Telegraph Hill at 3.30 p.m.

At 4 p.m. the brigade was ordered to a position of readiness west of Wancourt, on the report of the capture of that village. To get there it was necessary to come at a walk over shell-stricken ground, trenches, and wire, down a forward slope, in full view of the enemy until reaching the hollow south-west of Wancourt village. "C" Squadron were again sent on in advance of the brigade to prepare a track and reconnoitre the positions of our infantry. There was some shelling of the track, and "C" Squadron were shelled on the forward slope north-west of Wancourt, which was still held by the enemy. This first report and subsequent ones of the capture of Wancourt all proved false, and it is difficult to account for their persistence. Some light was thrown on the misunderstanding, however, when a tank which had just been round Neuville Vitasse reported on its return that it had been round Wancourt. Another contretemps occurred with a tank when Captain Scott first arrived with "C" Squadron in front of Wancourt. The officer in charge of a tank there got out and opened fire on him with an automatic pistol. Luckily, he used that weapon as unskilfully as most British officers.

"C" Squadron were lucky to come through the shelling with only two men wounded. When the regiment came on after them a timely snowstorm came on, hiding them from view, and they were not shelled. We remained in this hollow just behind the leading infantry in the tangled wire of the Hindenburg Line until 10 p.m. During this time Lieutenants Close, Trew, and Norman carried out useful patrols towards Monchy and Wancourt, both of which were held. A few horses were watered from shell-holes.

IN THE GREAT WAR

At 10 p.m. the Brigadier, General Bell-Smyth, having been given the choice of remaining there all night or of going back to water and feed and being in position again at 5 a.m. the next day, chose the latter alternative, and we went back to Ronville, arriving there at 12.30 a.m. There was much snow and it was bitterly cold, while men and horses had to remain in the open, dead-beat, no fires and very little to eat, all night.

11th April At 3.30 a.m. the Mobile Supply Column very luckily arrived with some oats, and about 6 lb. per horse was issued.

At 4 a.m. we returned to the position of the day before, but this time hidden behind the shoulder of the hill in front of Neuville Vitasse.

As soon as it grew light we could see the Scots Greys, who had remained out all night, being heavily shelled. They had a very bad time, and were withdrawn.

We were entirely unmolested, and at 12 noon the Brigade closed up to the east on persistent reports of the fall of Wancourt, while "D" Battery came into action. "C" Squadron was again sent forward at the head of the brigade, and at 1.30 p.m. Lieutenant Christie was sent forward with his troop to reconnoitre the west end of Wancourt, but found it strongly held by machine guns.

"C" Squadron did all the work done by the brigade during these two days, and did it very well.

At 3 p.m. we were ordered to Angy, leaving Lieutenant Trew with the infantry in front of Wancourt for liaison duties. On the march back it began to snow heavily again, and the horses were by now in a very bad state, eight dying. We bivouacked in the open in some one inch of snow, blowing half a gale. During the day the horses were not watered.

12th April On the 12th April at 1 p.m., detachments having come in, we marched to Gaudiempre. The horses were only just capable of moving, owing to lack of food, exposure, and exhaustion, while the men were little better.

THE 4TH (QUEEN'S OWN) HUSSARS

During these three days we had two men wounded and lost twenty-four horses—remarkably light casualties under the circumstances.

At Gaudiempre Major Mockett and Lieutenant Morrison, who had been doing liaison duty between the 2nd and 3rd Cavalry Division, rejoined, and Major Bell rejoined from " B " Echelon.

12th-18th April The 12th to the 18th were spent in billets. It was still cold, with rain and snow. The horses were in a very bad way, and there was some sickness amongst the men from trench feet and exposure. The Corps, Divisional and Brigade Commanders came round at intervals.

19th-20th April On the 19th and 20th we marched to Le Boisle, where the billets were much better. The weather remained cold until the 28th, when it grew warmer, and the horses improved. On the 28th the twenty-nine worst horses were cast. The horses of the regiment, however, did not properly recover from this expedition for a year.

11th May We remained in billets here until the 11th May, when the dismounted men left by lorry.

12th May On the 12th May and subsequent days the regiment marched via Wavans — Havernas — La Neuville—Suzanne to Marquaix.

18th May
19th May On the 18th the dismounted party of 300 went up to the trenches. On the 19th the horses were moved to bivouacs at Boucly.

The bivouacs and the trenches were in the devastated area. The bivouac was on high ground, and with summer weather was a very pleasant place to live in. There was endless grazing on very good crops of lucerne, clover, etc. There were no luxuries, such as estaminets or feminine society; but, on the other hand, there was a complete absence of crime of any kind.

The opposing trench lines were far apart, for the famous Hindenburg Line was behind the Canal du Nord, and our troops had not moved very near. The result was that the Germans had pushed out permanent outposts on our side of the canal, and we had run out corresponding advanced posts, but even these were in many places several hundred yards apart. In this wide No Man's Land was great scope for night patrols, but it was at the same time difficult to carry out raids, the distance of the opposing trenches making close observation—always necessary in planning a raid—almost impossible.

There were pleasant aspects about this form of warfare, however, for there was only shelling to fear—no mines, trench mortars, or bombs. Even the shelling was extremely light, and there were days when scarcely a shell was fired.

Our sector was on the left of the front allotted to the cavalry, and was in front of Pezieres. The system of holding the line was: Nearest the enemy a series of separate but mutually supporting posts, prepared for all-round defence. These were held night and day, but could be visited by day only at some risk, owing to their being overlooked by the enemy and there being no communication trenches. The terrain was open grass and of an undulating character.

Behind this came the real line of resistance—*i.e.*, K, L, and M posts. These were strong and were connected up by communication trenches, and were well garrisoned. Behind this line, again, were dug-outs in Pigeon Ravine and along a sunken lane called Fourteen Willows. Behind this was the village of Pezieres, destroyed by the enemy and shelled at times.

18th-21st May From the 18th to the 21st the regiment remained in support in Epehy, finding working parties for the trenches; no incidents. The 21st to the 24th: "A" Squadron in outpost line, "B" Squadron in M post, "C" Squadron in K and L posts.

A very quiet period; hardly a shot fired, but intermittent machine gunning by the enemy at night, intended, no doubt to catch ration parties, etc.

THE 4TH (QUEEN'S OWN) HUSSARS

24th May We were relieved on the night of the 24th. On this night Private Hall disappeared, and no more was heard of him for a very long time. He must have lost his way and walked into the German lines, for his grave was notified by them some months later. This was our only casualty.

26th-31st May On the 26th a working party of 200, under Major Bell, went up to near Ronssoy, and on the 30th a further 100 men were sent up to join them, and the whole went into the support line.

The new sector was similar to the last one held, except that the enemy trenches were a good deal nearer and it was not so quiet.

31st May During the night of 31st May–1st June the 4th Hussars relieved the 12th Lancers in the front line—namely, A, B, and C posts. These were mutually supporting, and covered 1,000 yards' frontage about 2,000 yards east of Ronssoy.

1st-3rd June On the 1st, 2nd and 3rd June there was only some light shelling, and patrols going out at night had no encounters.

4th June On the 4th General Greenly, commanding 2nd Cavalry Division, came up and said that an identification of the troops opposite to us was required, and we would probably have to make a raid the next time we were in the line.

5th June At about 1 a.m. on the 5th Sergeant Siddons, Corporal Bowstead, and two men went out on patrol. They encountered a hostile patrol of one officer and six men. These they attacked immediately. The officer was shot with a revolver, and one man was captured, being collared more or less simultaneously by the above-named N.C.Os. Captain Laing, who was commanding up there, was thus able to furnish the identification asked for with some promptness, and sent the man on to the division with the message: " Herewith identification as requested."

IN THE GREAT WAR

5th-6th June — The 5th and 6th were quiet. At 12.45 a.m. on the 7th the Germans put up a red rocket, bursting into two red balls; thirty seconds after a heavy bombardment opened on our posts, and a heavy barrage was put down behind. Enemy bombers then tried to get into our posts, but were repulsed in front of the wire. Our artillery S.O.S. barrage was good.

7th-14th June — The 7th was quiet, and that night we were relieved, going into support in the Quarries and Hardy Bank. This period to the 14th was very quiet.

It is impossible to give a detailed account of all the patrolling carried out as we had patrols out every night, but, with the exception of the instances given, no enemy was encountered.

14th June — The regiment took over the same front sector on the night of the 14th.

15th June The 15th was very quiet.

16th June — At 1 a.m. on the 16th a party of six Germans followed one of our patrols through our wire on the left of B post. They remained in the wire till our machine guns opened, and then ran. Privates Mason and Body went out to look for them, and found a German in a shell-hole, who surrendered without fighting. He was a Pole, and of a very low type. He stated he was one of fifty sent out to reconnoitre B post, and that the Germans were to attack it on

16th-18th June — the night of the 16th or 17th. Arrangements for a barrage were therefore made, and the line was strengthened with some Carabiniers up to the morning of the 18th, but no attack developed.

18th June — At 11.20 p.m. on the 18th a patrol of eight men ran into about fifty Germans to the left front of B post. A German fired a Véry light, and was shot. They then tried to surround our patrol, and wounded three of them. These were got in successfully, and the Germans then put up green lights, repeated in the Hindenburg Line to their rear.

THE 4TH (QUEEN'S OWN) HUSSARS

A heavy bombardment came down two minutes afterwards, to which our guns replied. The enemy never came up to our wire, but were close to it. They were driven off. This was undoubtedly intended for a raid, but our patrol presumably ran into the party as they were forming up.

19th-21st June — The 19th was quiet, but there was a good deal of shelling on the 20th on all our posts. On the 21st only intermittent shelling, and we were relieved that night.

During this tour in the line many patrols were out, Lieutenants France and Buddicom, of "B" Squadron, and Lieutenants Trew and Ash, of "C" Squadron, being out most nights. Lieutenant France and Corporal Bowstead one day crawled out into a German night post. An attempt to capture the occupants the following night was not successful.

Indian native cavalry were on our right, and were trench-mortared a good deal. It is a regrettable fact that certain of our snipers mistook some of them for Germans, but luckily had registered no hits before their mistake was pointed out.

22nd-26th June — On the 22nd there was an alarm in the early morning, owing to Guillemont Farm on our left being raided, but our troops were not employed. From that date to the 26th we had a quiet time in support in the Quarries.

27th June At 6 p.m. on the 27th the regiment's dismounted party moved to Pezieres, where "C" Squadron went into L, K, and M posts, two troops of "A" Squadron to Fourteen Willows, "B" Squadron and two troops of "A" Squadron to Pezieres. This was the same sector as that held from 18th to 26th May.

28th June — On the 28th we took over the outpost line, the remainder being in support in K, L, and M posts.

The outpost line was divided as follows :—One troop of "C" Squadron in No. 1 post, one troop of "C" Squadron in No. 2 post, one troop of "C" Squadron in sunken

1. A Corner of Ypres, 1915.
2. 1st Troop, "A" Squadron, resting on Canal north of Ypres the day after the first German gas attack.
3. "A" Squadron near Wargnies le Grand, August 29th, 1914.
4. "A" Squadron at Elouges, August 23rd, 1914.

road in rear of these posts, one troop of " C " Squadron and Headquarters in Quarry, one troop of " A " Squadron in No. 3 post, one troop of " A " Squadron in No. 4 post.

29th June The Diary for the 29th will give an idea of the trivial happenings in this portion of the line :—

" 5.30 a.m. : A few 77-mm. shells around Posts 3 and 4 from Honnecourt. A sniper appears to shoot from X.23.b.6.4, and a machine gun from X.23.b.8.2.

" 12 noon to 3 p.m. : Some 77-mm. shells around Nos. 3 and 4 posts. Ceased at 3 p.m. At 3.15 p.m. a German observer seen at X.23.b.6.3. At 7 p.m. information received that Germans in our front will be relieved to-night, when our guns would shell them at intervals. It was arranged to send out patrols during the intervals in the shelling " [which went out, but found the German outposts had withdrawn, and there were no encounters, though various observers' tracks and small trenches were found].

" At 7.45 p.m. to 8 p.m. the Quarry was shelled by 4·2's—1 per minute. Direction uncertain. Shells came at a very steep angle of descent.

" 9 p.m. : An enemy aeroplane came low over Quarry, firing a machine gun. Driven off by anti-aircraft guns."

30th June The next morning (30th June) was very quiet until 6.25 a.m., at which hour a very intense bombardment of the infantry trenches on our left began ; this included our Nos. 3 and 4 posts, but the shells luckily all fell between the posts and the Quarry. This lasted for twenty minutes, after which the enemy raided the infantry, but left a wounded German behind. They did not raid our posts, probably realizing they were held by us. As far as we were concerned the bombardment did us no harm, but many shells narrowly missed No. 3 post, and cut up the ground and cut all the wires around the Quarry.

1st-6th July The day was very quiet after that, and the next also. That night—1st July—" B " Squadron relieved " C " in the outpost line. All quiet to the 6th–7th, when we were partly relieved by infantry. On the 7th–8th relief was completed, three men being wounded just as they were moving off, one dying subsequently. Our total casualties from 1st June were four other ranks killed, twenty-three wounded.

Special Order, 2nd Cavalry Division.

" On the Division being relieved, I wish to express my admiration of the fighting qualities displayed and the amount of work done by all units during our tour in the trenches.

" As regards fighting, whether in attack or defence, opportunities of specially distinguishing themselves have happened to come more often to certain units than to others, but all have made the most of such chances as offered, and all have shown once again that our cavalry are fighting troops of the very first quality.

" Our complete superiority over the enemy has again been strongly emphasised.

" As regards work, my knowledge of the troops led me to expect a very large amount : I can only say that even those expectations were far surpassed by what was actually accomplished.

" I wish to congratulate all ranks of all units on their most successful and fruitful efforts, staffs, services, and departments no less than regiments and batteries.

" W. H. Greenly, *Major-General,*
" 8th July, 1917."   " *Commanding 2nd Cavalry Division.*"

" My dear Darley,

" In a Division like this it is very difficult to single out any particular regiment for special praise ; but I wish to let you know that I think the work done by the 4th Hussars has been particularly good. The spirit of offence and the morale of the regiment generally have been very prominent, and the example of the

IN THE GREAT WAR

officers in much excellent and bold patrolling has been altogether admirable.

"I should be glad if you would convey to all ranks my high appreciation of what they have achieved.

"Yours sincerely,

"W. H. GREENLY."

7th-13th July On relief the dismounted party rejoined the horses at Boucly, and the next few days were spent in cleaning up, etc.

13th July to 11th Sept. On the 13th the regiment marched, and on the 17th reached Rebreuviette—somewhat restricted billets. Here we remained until the 11th September. During this period much mounted training was carried out, and horse shows were a popular feature.

On the 20th June Captain Evans had finished his time as Adjutant, and Lieutenant Christie took over the duties.

11th Sept. to 8th Oct. On the 11th billets were moved to Vacquerie-le-Boucq; "A" Squadron in Boubers, "B" in Fortel, "C" in Ligny and Petit Boubers. These were much better billets, with good cover for horses.

On the 13th the dismounted men were reduced to thirty, and fifty were sent to join the infantry.

On the 23rd a working party of Lieutenants Trew, Pegrum, and Ede, with 110 other ranks, was sent to join the 5th Cavalry Brigade dismounted battalion for work round Mazingarbe.

8th-20th Oct. Training was carried on with the remainder until the 8th October, when another move was made to St. Michel-sur-Ternoise, etc. During this time Captain Beaman, D.S.O., joined from the Indian Cavalry, and also Second-Lieutenants Graham and Malcolm. A working party of two officers and fifty-nine other ranks proceeded to an area east of Peronne on the 19th to construct horse shelters; they were subsequently joined by the party which had gone to Mazingarbe.

20th-22nd Oct. On the 20th marched to Vacquerie-le-Boucq, 21st to Berteaucourt, 22nd to an area near Amiens, consisting of Ailly-sur-Somme, Dreuil, Montieres, and Saveuse.

2nd-Lieutenants Quinlan, Smith, C. E. Christie, and Howe joined here. The working party had seven men slightly gassed on the 6th and 7th near Lens.

22nd Oct. to 16th Nov. The regiment remained in these billets until the 16th November. On that date we marched to Bray. The general impression was that we were going to occupy the huts and stables recently erected in the devastated area for the winter.

On the 17th marched to the huts at Trefcon.

19th Nov. On the night of the 19th orders were received for the attack on Cambrai. This was the first intimation received of any impending attack, though in former attacks even regimental officers knew long beforehand of what was going to occur. The orders issued were very ambitious—e.g., "A" Squadron was ordered to go through to Escadœuvres, north of Cambrai, by the evening of the first day, a distance of twenty-nine miles as the crow flies.

20th Nov. At 1.45 a.m. on the 20th the regiment marched via Roisel to St. Emilie and watered there, and then halted near Villers Faucon. At 6.20 a.m. the battle opened with a deafening bombardment, to which the Germans appeared to reply but feebly.

At 11.15 a.m. the regiment started, and advanced via Gouzeaucourt to the hill three miles south of Masnieres. We had in front of us here the 5th Cavalry Brigade, while the Canadian Brigade and the 5th Cavalry Division were in front of them. The battle had gone wonderfully well up to a point, but the Canal du Nord proved to be too hard a nut to crack, and only one squadron of Canadian cavalry got over.

IN THE GREAT WAR

20th-21st Nov. The regiment halted here, watering from shell-holes, until 3.30 p.m. on the 21st, and then moved back to Villers Faucon. Here we remained until 5.15 p.m.
23rd Nov. on the 23rd, and then moved very hurriedly to just
24th Nov. north of Fins. On the night of the 24th fresh operation orders were issued for the next day; these, again, were very ambitious. To take an example: "A" Squadron, after Bourlon village had been taken, was to advance through it and occupy a farm some miles beyond it; they would be unsupported there, and after arrival there appeared
25th Nov. to be no orders as to the next action to be taken.

At 7 a.m. the brigade marched to a point one mile north-west of Ribecourt, and halted there in full view of the Germans east of Masnieres. At about 11 a.m. enemy field guns opened fire, but only a few of them, and we were able to edge away until out of sight in a dip in the ground.

We remained here until 5 p.m. without being molested, and were then ordered to leave a dismounted party and find the Headquarters for the dismounted brigade party under Lieutenant-Colonel Darley, while the horses were sent back to Fins, which was reached long after dark.

26th Nov. The dismounted party remained at Ribecourt for the night, and at 4 p.m. on the 26th moved to dug-outs on the road running due north from Havrincourt, and about two miles due north of it.

27th Nov. At 6 p.m. on the 27th the party moved to Bourlon Wood to take over the line held by the 2/7th West Yorks, under the command of Brigadier-General Bradshaw.

28th Nov. The relief was completed by 3.15 a.m., the 4th Hussars being on the right sector—5th Cavalry Brigade on their right, 16th Lancers on their left, 5th Lancers in support.

THE 4TH (QUEEN'S OWN) HUSSARS

The line ran along the northern edge of the wood, about 200 yards inside it, facing the village of Bourlon, still held by the Germans, though there were said to be some men of the Highland Light Infantry still in it. The general confusion of the situation was extreme, all sorts of units being mixed up all over the wood; while it was also full of German snipers, and was shelled pretty continuously with gas shells. The remaining hours of darkness were spent in digging, and it was as well that this was done, for the shelling the next day was heavy. Lieutenant Fisher-Smith, the signalling officer, was killed at 1 p.m.; and the 22nd Royal Fusiliers in support lost heavily, as did the 12th Lancers on the right.

The shelling went on continuously up to 8 p.m., when the 4th and 5th Dismounted Battalions were relieved by infantry, the 4th Hussars coming into support. Here again the enemy shelled steadily all night, chiefly gas and lachrymatory shells.

29th Nov. Early on the 29th Captain Scott was wounded, and lost the sight of the left eye. The S.O.S. signal was sent up at 7.30 a.m. on the right of the line, but no attack materialized, though shelling went on all day more or less severely. That night the regiment was relieved by infantry, and moved back to Flesquieres and rested till the next

30th Nov. day, when the horses were picked up at Beaucamp and the party returned to Fins at a pace as near a gallop as could be worked up in the heavy traffic.

This was due to the enemy having broken through at dawn north of Epehy, at the place where the regiment had been in the line in July, 1917. They had completely surprised the garrison, and reached Gouzeaucourt about 10 a.m. Here they stopped, largely in order to loot the canteen there, and were driven out by the Guards.

Fins and vicinity was shelled by high velocity guns as soon as the attack commenced, and there were many stragglers pouring through it a few hours afterwards.

IN THE GREAT WAR

As soon as our dismounted party got in the regiment stood-to, and at 5.30 p.m. was moved to a position of readiness south-east of Desart Wood, but at 8.15 p.m. was recalled to camp and off-saddled.

1st Dec. The next day there was still a feeling of insecurity in the air, but the Germans seemed to have somewhat over-reached themselves, and were losing heavily all along the front of attack. Fins was shelled by high velocity guns.

2nd-4th Dec. From the 2nd to the 4th December remained in camp, finding working parties for trenches near Gouzeaucourt. The weather all this time was bitterly cold, while we had only a few tents, thus causing some sickness.

4th Dec. On the 4th a dismounted party went up to Vaucelette Farm, near Villers Guislain, and took over the line.

5th Dec. The night and next day passed without incident, and at 8 p.m. they returned. Meanwhile, the camp was considerably shelled by large calibre high velocity guns, but, very luckily, no casualties were incurred. Enemy aircraft also dropped a number of bombs very near the lines without killing anyone.

6th-8th Dec. On the 6th marched to huts at Brusle. On the 7th to Sailly-le-Sec; on the 8th to Prouzel, Plachy-Buyon, and Fossemanant.

20th-28th Dec. Remained here until the 20th December, when a dismounted party left for the front line. This party were in reserve in Vendelles until the 28th, during which time many working parties were found for the front line as far away as Villeret—a very long distance, which made a night's work a very strenuous business. The weather was vile, with some heavy snowstorms. Christmas Eve, when most of the party was out working, was a very unpleasant night, snowing heavily and blowing a gale.

THE 4TH (QUEEN'S OWN) HUSSARS

28th Dec. On the 28th moved up to Côte Wood for three very quiet days, during which time there was practically no shelling.

1st Jan., 1918. At midnight on the 31st December we saw the New Year in while marching to the front line before Villeret. There was a No Man's Land of 100-300 yards, but the Germans held their front line very weakly by day. Our wire was not very strong. It froze terribly hard the night of the 1st January, and " C " Squadron, who were in the open in a support trench, had a very cold time of it.

2nd Jan. On the night of the 2nd two patrols, under Lieutenants Quinlan and Coghlan, went out to reconnoitre the enemy's front line. They went out from opposite ends and met on the enemy's wire, who spotted them and bombed and opened rifle fire on them, wounding one man. The next day we got a trench mortar on to a machine gun located the night before, and it fired no more. The enemy retaliated with a few rifle grenades.

2nd-5th Jan. All this tour, which ended on the 5th, was very quiet, and at night we patrolled No Man's Land without opposition. On the night of the 5th returned to Vendelles in a thaw, the roads being a sheet of ice.

8th-11th Jan. The regiment remained in reserve until the 11th, finding working parties every night as before. They then moved up to Côte Wood again in support, and

11th-16th Jan. remained there until the 16th, being intermittently shelled, three other ranks being killed and four wounded.

On the night of the 16th moved up to the same trenches in front of Villeret, which were in a bad state owing to the rapid thaw after severe frost. As before, many patrols went out, and did much as they liked in No Man's Land at first. Later the enemy were more alert and wounded three men. One of the latter was with Lieutenant Morrison, who brought him back all the way

IN THE GREAT WAR

from the German wire, being awarded the Military Cross for this action.

23rd-27th Jan. On the 23rd "A" and "C" Squadrons went into reserve in Priel Wood, "B" Squadron to Hetty Post, until the 27th, when they were relieved by native cavalry, returning to billets at Prouzel on the 28th.

3rd Feb. On the 3rd February the regiment marched to St. Christ, arriving there on the night of the 4th. This was a village on the Somme on the edge of the old Somme battlefield, and it was interesting to explore the old trenches. The country was entirely devastated, but comfortable huts and stables had been put up, and with football, etc., the time passed pleasantly. The much advertised great German offensive was expected to start any day, and most of this period was spent standing-to ready to move. All officers reconnoitred the front line and the various routes to it and intermediate lines. A considerable amount of training was also carried out. The various lines of defence did not inspire people with much confidence, many of them being largely imaginary owing to lack of labour to dig them.

Many officers were away on courses during all this winter, especially at the 2nd Divisional Tactical School, started by Major Mockett, 4th Hussars, in the end of 1916, and commanded at this time by Major Laing, 4th Hussars. During the second week in March the regiment moved to Grandru, where numerous rumours of the Huns' pending offensive were rife.

CHAPTER IX

21st MARCH—22nd JULY, 1918

THE GREAT GERMAN OFFENSIVE.

21st Mar. This was a red-letter day for the Fifth Army. The Hun bombardment started at about 4 a.m., and when dawn broke it was so foggy that one could not see more than about twenty yards. News soon came through that the long-expected great Hun offensive had started, and we heard of positions being lost along the whole Army front. The 4th Brigade dismounted battalion embussed at about midday and went off. Major Laing returned at 1 p.m. from the Tactical School at Bussy-les-Daours. Orders came for the 3rd Brigade dismounted battalion to embus at 2.30 p.m. The 4th Hussars company was commanded by Lieutenant R. J. V. Falkner, M.C., the other officers to go up being Lieutenant W. D. Buddicom 2nd-Lieutenant K. J. Malcolm, Lieutenant M. S. Close, and Lieutenant C. G. Norman.

22nd Mar. Another very foggy morning. News came through that the 3rd Corps had withdrawn its whole line to their battle positions. We had no news of our dismounted party, and it remained thick all day. During the evening swarms of Hun aeroplanes crossed us on their way to bomb Compiegne. It was really very amusing to see the Labour battalions and Chinese coolies trekking westwards. They had never before done such a day's work in their lives!

IN THE GREAT WAR

23rd Mar. A very fine morning. Brigadier-General Bell-Smyth, C.M.G., who had been up to the front, came back and reported that the fighting was very hot, and that our troops had been heavily engaged. At about 10 a.m. a further party of thirty-three men, under Captain M. F. Radclyffe, went up mounted. Their action is described in the report written by Captain Radclyffe :—

" On the 22nd March a mixed mounted squadron from each brigade in the Division came under the command of Captain Bonham, Scots Greys, near Guiscard. Each squadron was about 110 strong. I commanded the 3rd Brigade squadron. We moved to Berlancourt as reserve.

" The situation along the whole front Ham—Jussy was very vague and practically unknown.

" Captain Bonham was first sent with the three squadrons to Ugny-le-Gay, with orders to take up a defensive position in Bois de Genlis. We arrived at the village late at night, and sent patrols to reconnoitre the ground to our objective, but later received orders to withdraw to Les Hezettes, where we spent the night. At 6 a.m., 23rd March, we returned to Berlancourt into Corps reserve. Protective patrols were put out in the direction of Ham. About midday it was reported that Ham was in German hands, also Esmery-Hallon, and that they were advancing south from the latter, but the situation was still very obscure. Captain Bonham received orders to reconnoitre and, if possible, clear up the situation towards Esmery-Hallon, also to move the regiment to Bois de l'Hopital and assist the troops there if necessary.

" On arrival at the north-east corner of Bois de l'Hopital we found mixed detachments of French and British troops holding a line (partly dug in) of posts in front of Flavy-le-Meldeux and Bois de l'Hopital. These troops were very unsteady, and the British mixed force seemed to have hardly any officers. There was little or no organization, and no prepared lines.

THE 4TH (QUEEN'S OWN) HUSSARS

"We were under machine-gun fire from Esmery-Hallon, and troops of the Scots Greys trying to get a footing in the village were driven back.

"The French commander at Ferme du Bois Brule withdrew our regiment into reserve at the farm, and late that evening we were preparing to return to Corps Headquarters at Berlancourt when a heavy machine-gun and artillery fire was directed by the enemy on the north end of the Bois de l'Hopital, held by the French. I was sent with a patrol (two men) to find out and report the situation. In the wood I met French infantry withdrawing. On reaching the north end of the wood I found heavy fighting in progress. One or two French machine guns were still holding on, but the enemy had got a footing in the wood. I returned and reported, and it was decided to counter-attack with our cavalry regiment (dismounted). Later an order arrived from a higher French Commander for us to fall back and hold Ferme de Rouvrel, with French on our left and British on our right.

"I was ordered to hold for the night a line of outposts in front of the farm with the squadron, the reserve squadrons being behind the farm.

"I got touch with the French and British troops on my left and right, and tried to keep it during the night. I had eight Hotchkiss rifles, and put four well forward and four in a second line, with my troop posts all dug in farther back. No serious fighting took place, but the British troops from Flavy kept coming through us, saying they had been relieved. There was a dense fog, and it was difficult to see and to keep up inter-communication.

"At dawn we lost touch with the infantry, and my patrols going to Flavy were driven in by hostile fire. The enemy, being unopposed, were working round our right. At this time the French withdrew, and we were ordered back to Catigny, where we joined another mounted detachment under Colonel Cook, and came under his orders on the 25th March."

IN THE GREAT WAR

In the afternoon the remainder of the regiment and transport moved to Lagache. Hostile aeroplanes were again very busy at night " laying their eggs."

24th Mar. A beautiful day. In the morning a few men rejoined us. A move was then made to Bailly, and in the evening spare horses were sent off, under Second-Lieutenant W. C. Bailey, to bring back the original dismounted company, who left Grandru on the 21st. As a matter of fact, these horses were all taken by Lieutenant-Colonel Cook, D.S.O., 20th Hussars, to mount other men of the Division, and so make up a mounted force. This force did good service at the Battle of Lagny, the following report of which is supplied by Captain M. F. Radclyffe :—

" On the morning of the 26th March the Divisional Mounted Force was at H.15 under Colonel Cook. Each brigade was about two squadrons strong. The line was reported to run B.18.b—C.20 central—C.27—I.4. A gap in the line was reported between Lagny and Bois des Essarts, and Colonel Cook's force was ordered to fill it.

" Verbal orders were given to—
   3rd Brigade Squadron to seize and hold ridge at C.25.c.
   4th Brigade Squadron to seize and hold Ferme Charbonneaux.

" The ridge between Dives and Plessis was being shelled.

" I detailed a squadron as advanced guard, directed on the brigade objectives (high ground at C.25.c.), and followed in close support with the other squadron. Squadrons moved over ridge in shell formation, the leading squadron with one troop out in front.

" As the Germans were attacking and the French vague about the situation, I sent a troop to C.19.d.2.3., with a standing patrol at C.19 central. This patrol reported the French withdrawing about C.19. I immediately sent the remainder of reserve squadron to C.19.d.2.3, with a troop at C.19 central, and reported my action to Colonel Cook, who was with Reserve Brigade behind Ferme Charbonneaux. He sent me a squadron of the 20th Hussars. As the situation developed and the French gave way in Lagny, it later became necessary to put this squadron in the line at C.25.b.2.8. My orders were to hold on at all costs. He also sent a squadron of the Scots Greys to C.19.c.

"The Germans, following their usual tactics, pushed round the flanks, and, making great use of the ground to push forward their automatic rifles, got a footing in Bois des Essarts, and advanced rapidly through the wood.

"The French then gave way north of the Scots Greys at C.19.a, allowing the enemy to push rapidly through Montagne-de-Lagny, and so compelled the Scots Greys to withdraw. At the same time the French withdrew from Lagny.

"Colonel Cook then gave me orders to hold on till he had withdrawn from Ferme Charbonneaux, and then withdraw my three squadrons, which were now heavily engaged.

"The led horses of the Division were kept very close up and were shelled frequently, many being killed and a number breaking away.

"We withdrew by squadrons under heavy machine-gun fire from three sides, and consequently lost a good number in wounded and a few prisoners.

"No positions in rear were prepared, and although some resistance was put up on the ridge about H.11, the force was withdrawn to Thiescourt, from where the French troops (the first really serviceable-looking troops we had met during the retreat) arrived and took over.

"The cavalry was collected and taken to Elincourt for the night, and thence to Compiegne on the 27th March."

IN THE GREAT WAR

25th Mar.   A fine morning after a very frosty night. Captain A. A. H. Beaman, D.S.O. (1st Indian Cavalry), attached 4th Hussars, was ordered to take further spare horses up to the battle. He also took Lieutenant F. A. Sykes, Lieutenant F. H. Ash, Lieutenant W. T. Pegrum, Lieutenant H. D. Quinlan, 2nd-Lieutenant R. W. Howe, and 2nd-Lieutenant A. D. J. Brennan. The action of this force in the Bois des Essarts is described in the following report of Captain Beaman :—

" A composite squadron, 125 strong, including 75 other ranks of the dismounted trench party, picked up and mounted *en route*, formed a squadron of the 3rd Brigade Regiment, under Colonel Brooke, 16th Lancers.

" We bivouacked on the night of 25th–26th March at Chiry. About 8 a.m. on the 26th Colonel Brooke gave orders to march at once via Suzoy and counter-attack Porquericourt. Order of march: 16th Lancers, 4th Hussars, 5th Lancers. Shortly afterwards the enemy was reported holding Bois de la Reserve, so the march was directed on that objective. The 16th Lancers formed an advanced guard; 4th Hussars put out flank guards of one section to each flank. The Bois de la Reserve was found to be unoccupied, so the regiment was moved up to about I.19.a.89. Colonel Brooke, believing Bois des Clochettes to be only very lightly held, ordered me to take it with the 4th Hussars squadron—mounted if possible.

" This knoll was surrounded by wire and trenches; my patrols could find no gaps, so I dismounted in the sunken road H.18.d.50, and advanced in the wood with three troops, the remaining troop being away on flank guard and patrols.

" On arrival at north slope of wood I could see French troops on the slope north of Guy, and our advanced guard (16th Lancers) debouching from the north of Guy, so I mounted and followed on, leaving out a patrol to keep touch with the 3rd Cavalry Division on our left. Joined up in rear of 5th Lancers just south of Guy. Regiment halted and dismounted for about an hour at I.7.c.7.8.

THE 4TH (QUEEN'S OWN) HUSSARS

There was some slight crumping and machine gunning from north-east. Colonel Brooke told me that the Canadian Brigade was rounding up about thirty Boches in the Bois des Essarts, and ordered me to advance along the north edge of the wood to the road running from I.2 central to I.15 central and join up with the Canadians.

"Advanced in the following formation:—

"Two troops in line with scouts, and two troops in support in column.

"After previous experience, I ordered that the squadron front from the north edge of the wood should not exceed fifty yards. The two support troops followed under me in close touch at less than 50 yards. Just as we were starting into the wood, S.S.M. Baron reported to me from our left flank patrol that the French had retired and the 3rd Cavalry Division were being driven back. I sent him to report to the O.C. I had with me a runner from each troop and a Regimental Headquarters runner. Even at these short distances and intervals touch was difficult to maintain, and progress was slow.

"Lieutenant Quinlan went on to liaise with Canadian Headquarters at the chateau.

"During our advance the wood was swept by a machine-gun barrage, which, however, went high. The inside of the wood was rifle-grenaded and the north edge crumped.

"The advance to the objective was about 1,000 yards.

"When we were nearing it Lieutenant Quinlan returned with a verbal message from O.C. Canadians to say that he was holding the road, our objective, but was very anxious about his left flank —*i.e.*, the north edge of the wood. I replied that I would hold that, and sent a message to Colonel Brooke, repeating the O.C. Canadians' message, and saying that I would take on the north edge of the wood as far as I could westward from the road.

"Meanwhile the 1st troop had lost its direction, so, to save time, I wheeled the 3rd Troop into line along the edge of the

IN THE GREAT WAR

wood, and sent runners to the other troops, telling the 1st Troop to wheel round and line the edge of the wood, and the 4th and 2nd to come into support.

"It is instructive to note that, owing to the noise, the heavy fire down open rides, and the thickness of the other parts of the wood, it took at least half an hour before this movement began to take place. Meanwhile the 3rd Troop was in position along the edge of the wood. Parties of the enemy kept appearing on the slope about 400 yards north with automatic rifles, but these were easily kept down by our rifle fire, and showed no inclination to advance. Presently the flank scouts of the 3rd Troop, where I was, came and reported that there were Germans in the wood about 100 yards to our right rear. I could catch glimpses of them through my glasses, but, believing the Canadians to be holding the road, I thought they must be French, so we went on a little to make sure. They were a party of about ten Germans advancing straight down the road. A few shots stopped them, but away to their left more were coming on, shouting and crashing through the wood. A runner then told me that the Canadians had run short of ammunition and retired from the wood, and that our other three troops were being driven back through the wood. Situation like this :—

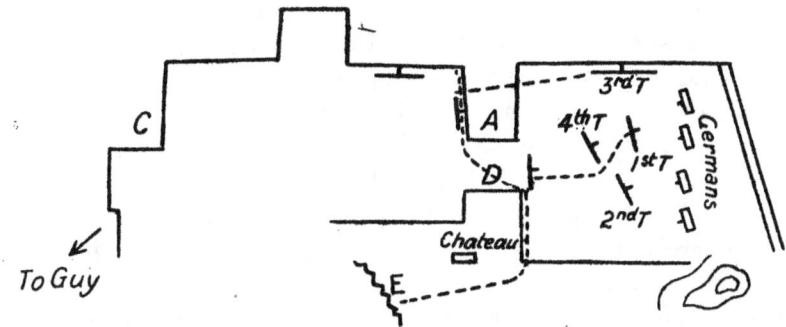

"I decided to retire across ride *A*, so as to check Germans as they came across the open; did so rapidly. Germans also firing from ridge 400 yards north of wood. Placed half troop to keep down automatic gunners on ridge, other half along bank on track (*vide* sketch) to catch them as they came into open in *A*. A few minutes later a runner from led horses (Private Gibson) arrived and reported that the 5th and 16th Lancers had retired to Guy, and the Germans were entering the wood at *C*. Decided to get out of it to the chateau (where I expected to find the Canadians) with all speed. Joined Lieutenant Howe with 1st Troop at *D*. He informed me that other troops had gone back, so with these two troops followed the edge of the wood up to the chateau grounds. The Canadians had gone, but just south of the chateau were large numbers of 3rd Hussars. Parties of these joined me, and I took up a position in a trench a few hundred yards south-west of the chateau. When the Germans tried to come out of the wood towards the chateau, we opened Hotchkiss and rifle fire on them. They instantly fled back into the wood, leaving some dead and wounded in the open. It was always possible to locate the German front line, as they fired up Véry lights, and a few minutes after these lights going up a barrage of field guns and 4·2-inch howitzers came down about 150 yards to 200 yards ahead. The enemy made no further attempts to advance from the chateau direction, but lights were going up from north base of the hill in I.10.20, and also away to our left, north-west of Bois des Clochettes.

"Anxious about the two dominating peaks on our right and left rear, and also as there was a long belt of wire behind us with only one gap, I retired along a sunken lane, through the wire, and took up a position with 3rd and 4th Hussars along the ridge I.13.c.3.5., which commanded the belt of wire. There Lieutenant Pargiter and a troop of 16th Lancers joined up with us. We remained here about half an hour while I tried to discover what was on our right and left. The Germans made no further advance on our front; the hill on our right was reported unoccupied, the hill on the left obscure; and it was reported that the Canadians, 16th and 5th Lancers, and remainder of 4th Hussars had gone off mounted in a south-west direction. This meant that our flanks were in the air. Just then Colonel Brooke arrived with the led horses, mounted the 3rd Hussars on spare horses, and took the party mounted to about H.30.b. central. Colonel Brooke was then called away. I dismounted, took up a position, and sent out to get touch with nearest troops. None could be found on our left; the 5th Cavalry Brigade was reported on our right. Mounted and moved on to join up with them. Found a small party of Scots Greys holding a bank about H.27.c.0.5.; put 4th Hussars in to strengthen them. There was a strong trench line, well wired, facing north-west, running along ridge in H.31-32, forming defensive flank and securing crossing of stream; put 3rd Hussars in there. Led horses over the stream to Ville. Went on to Dive le Franc to report dispositions to Divisional Headquarters. Found Colonel Brooke there and handed back command. We remained in those positions for the night, and were relieved by French infantry at 8 a.m. on 27th. Lieutenant Pegrum rejoined next day, and reported that he had done a rearguard at Guy, covering the mounted retirement of 16th Lancers."

Second-Lieutenant W. C. Bailey returned with a few of our men, and reported that the rest of the horses he took up had been taken by Colonel Cook, 20th Hussars, to make a mounted force. The remains of the original dismounted company, which left on the 21st March, rejoined. Standing-to all night. Compiegne very heavily bombed during the night.

26th Mar. Moved at 7.30 a.m. through the woods and through Compiegne into a wood on the west side. Heard that Noyon had fallen to the Germans on the previous night, and we could see it burning. Numerous reports came in as to what was going on, but they were very disjointed, as there were two battles in which our men were engaged—*i.e.*, Battle of Lagny (*see* Captain Radclyffe's report) and the Battle of Bois des Essarts (*see* Captain Beaman's report).

THE 4TH (QUEEN'S OWN) HUSSARS

27th Mar. In the afternoon all the parties which had been away rejoined, and we had about an hour to sort ourselves out. The Hun offensive had been stopped in this part of the front, and it is interesting to know that he never made any further progress. The French then took over, and the remnants of the Division were able to collect. Later the regiment went into bivouac at Moyvillers.

28th Mar. During the night a message came through that the Germans had captured Montdidier, and were marching westwards down the road towards Beauvais, so we were ordered to march at 7 a.m. to the woods near Montgerain, and then on to Plainville. "B" Echelon was ordered to park and defend Moyvillers. "B" Squadron, under Captain Radclyffe, was advanced squadron. The inhabitants were very afraid, and had no idea of the proximity of the Hun. There were no doubt many enemy agents riding round the country on bicycles, trying to cause a panic. We soon found that the story of the Hun march on Beauvais was not true, although he had captured Montdidier; but a counter-attack by French reserves, who were sent up by lorry, stopped him coming farther than about a mile west of Montdidier. The regiment went on to Plainville, and remained in the vicinity of the village for the rest of the day. Having got into touch with the French and found out the situation, a dismounted battalion was ordered to put Plainville in a state of defence. Lieutenant-Colonel J. E. Darley was in command, with Major N. O. Laing as second-in-command.

Lieutenant J. D. Delius was acting Adjutant throughout these operations, as Captain A. H. Christie, M.C., was sick. No break had occurred, but the presence of British troops was requested by the French Commander to keep up the moral of his troops. The rest of the brigade and all the horses went to Chapoix, in the valley farther west, where there was water for them. Work on the defence of Plainville was carried out that night, but it poured with rain, and not much work could be done, owing to the late hour at which orders were given.

29th Mar. There had been no attack during the night, and the French seemed to be steadier. In point of fact, the Hun never advanced any farther at this point of the line. After further work on Plainville defences, the horses suddenly appeared at about midday, and orders were given to join the rest of the brigade at Chapoix. It was then found that the Germans were pressing on hard farther north, and that Amiens was in imminent danger. Having filled nosebags and got some bully and biscuits, the whole brigade marched north to Cottenchy, where we arrived just before dusk and went into bivouac.

30th Mar. Started off in a great hurry at 8 a.m. via Paraclet to Thiennes. Divisional Headquarters was at Boves.

The situation was very vague until we got to Windmill Hill. It was then found that the Canadian Brigade, under General Seely, had attacked and got a footing in Cavalry Wood just above Moreuil. General Bell-Smyth at once gave orders to the brigade, and the 4th Hussars were on the extreme right. The detail of the action of the 2nd Cavalry Division with the Canadian Brigade on the 30th March and the 1st April will be found in the official report by the " G " Staff of the Division (*see* Appendix A).

" A " Squadron, 4th Hussars, under Lieutenant G. Greville, was ordered to work down the western edge of the Bois de Moreuil, and to secure the right flank of the Canadians. This squadron got a footing on the ridge between Moreuil and the wood, and sent patrols through Moreuil village to gain touch with the French. Corporal Stapley and Lance-Corporal Sampson of " A " Squadron, and Corporal Law of " B " Squadron, all did excellent work here with their patrols. Moreuil was now being shelled by both sides. " A " Squadron was in front of the general alignment on the left, and as a result came under heavy machine-gun fire from the southwest corner of the wood; their led horses, too, were shelled by the French, who mistook them for Uhlan horses. Several Hun horses were captured in Moreuil village. " A " Squadron were forced to retire from the ridge they had been holding, but there was another about half a mile north, on which " B " Squadron were, and who covered the retirement. Meanwhile " C " Squadron under Captain Beaman, were ordered to work along the western edge of the wood. Having reached a track at I.3.b.6.4, they got in touch with the right of the Canadians. They received verbal orders from General Seely to push on to the corner of the wood (*i.e.*, the same corner from which the fire made " A " Squadron withdraw). They met very heavy and accurate machine-gun and field-gun fire, and had to withdraw to the track. Squadrons of 5th and 16th Lancers and some men of the Warwicks reinforced the line in the wood, which was slightly advanced. Very heavy fighting went on all day, and the casualties were heavy. The line was finally taken over by the 8th Infantry Division at 2.30 a.m. on the 31st, and the regiment withdrew to Thiennes. It had been pouring with rain all day. Colonel Darley was riding his horse " Bill " when a shell pitched right under him; fortunately, it was a " dud." Major Laing was saved by his steel helmet, a machine-gun bullet hitting it and denting it sufficiently to knock him out, and slightly wounding him; he, however, remained with the regiment. During the day two machine guns of the 3rd Machine Gun Squadron were at the disposal of the C.O.; and " D " Battery, R.H.A., under Major Norton, was also available, although no favourable targets appeared.

31st Mar. A fine day and a reasonably quiet morning. The horses were kept saddled up, and we were ready to move instantly. At about 1 p.m. an urgent message came from General Bell-Smyth, ordering the regiment to gallop up to Windmill Hill and get into dismounted action, as the infantry of the 8th Division had been driven out of Moreuil Wood. All three squadrons were dismounted, as the ground was quite unsuitable for any mounted action. Rapid fire was at once opened, range 900 yards, at the Germans, who were debouching from the western edge of the wood. This at once stopped them, and they could be seen running back to the wood or digging in in the open. The Hotchkiss rifles did good work in silencing the enemy automatic weapons, and " D " Battery did some very pretty execution at a good target. Later on squadrons of the 5th and 16th Lancers came into the alignment. Owing to the lie of the country, both " A " and " C " Squadrons had to go farther forward than " B " Squadron to get their field of fire. In the evening the enemy captured Rifle Wood, on our left, and were able to bring enfilade machine-gun fire on "A" and " C " Squadrons, and heavy casualties were caused. Colonel Darley was riding near the Brigadier, when again a shell pitched right under his horse; unfortunately, it was not a " dud," and the horse " Bill " and Colonel Darley were killed instantly. He was buried later at Thiennes. Major Laing then took over command of the regiment. Having no entrenching tools on the men these had to be sent back for from the tool packs with the led horses, which were below Windmill Hill. Extra ammunition had also to be got up. By nightfall the casualties had become very heavy, but the remainder of the men dug themselves in well. The Hotchkiss gun numbers had had very heavy losses. The squadrons remained in their positions all night. The horses were moved back about two miles to where they could water and get forage. The night passed off quietly.

1st April Rifle Wood having been lost, it was necessary to counter-attack it, so General Bell-Smyth went to Divisional Headquarters at about 1 a.m. He then had a conference of all C.Os. at 5 a.m. The plan of the attack is as shown in the report written by " G." 2nd Cavalry Division (*see* Appendix B). The 3rd Brigade, having lost very heavily, could take no part in the actual attack, but protected the right flank of it. The attack was successful, and, apart from shelling, the rest of the day was quiet. We heard we were to be relieved during the night by the 2nd Rifle Brigade. When they arrived we found

THE 4TH (QUEEN'S OWN) HUSSARS

Major A. E. Wass, M.C., a 4th Hussar, in command of the battalion. The whole line was taken over by the 14th (British) Division and the French 33rd Division. This line also remained practically the same until the August offensive, except that the French lost some ground, which enabled the Hun to shell the Amiens—Paris railway, and so suspend all traffic. The final relief took place at 2.30 a.m., and we got back to our horses, and then on to Cottenchy, where we arrived, very tired, at 4.30 a.m.

2nd April After a few hours' sleep the regiment moved down to Paraclet, where we bivouacked. The squadrons sorted themselves out as best they could, and refitted with ammunition and Hotchkiss rifles. Major Evans, M.C., and 2nd-Lieutenant Bailey rejoined. Everybody had a welcome sleep. Things seemed pretty quiet; the Hun had been successfully stopped, having got to the limit of his offensive in this part of the line. There is no doubt that the 2nd Cavalry Division and the Canadian Mounted Brigade played a great part in the successful defence of Amiens.

3rd April The regiment marched at 10.30 a.m. via Amiens to Camon, where it arrived about noon. Everybody was very sorry to hear of the death of Brigadier-General Charles Campbell, 16th Lancers, which took place at Tréport. He had been commanding the 5th Brigade for some while. The " B " Echelon arrived in the afternoon, and we were all glad to get a change of clothing. Major A. D. Bell came up to the regiment, having been sick in England for some while.

4th April A very wet morning. The first real shelling of Amiens started. In the afternoon we got " C " Squadron of the Leicestershire Yeomanry as reinforcements, with horses. These were very welcome, as we had been sadly depleted. In the evening " B " Echelon went off towards Longpré with Major Bell. Major Laing was informed he was to remain in command of the regiment. Still very wet.

MAJOR (TEMP. LIEUT.-COL.) N. O. LAING, D.S.O.,
who commanded the 4th Hussars from April 2, 1918, to the return in May 1919.

IN THE GREAT WAR

5th April The situation to the east of Amiens was at this time still precarious, and very heavy fighting was going on.

It was about this time that General Carey, who was returning from England, collected all the men he could find, and put up such a splendid show about Villers-Bretonneux. Sergeant Millest, 4th Hussars, was one of the party, and received a Military Medal afterwards. The regiment moved off at 7 a.m., and got as far as Picquigny, when it was stopped owing to the tactical situation. After some delay, and having watered and fed the horses, the regiment went into bivouac at La Chaussée-Tirancourt, across the river, where we remained at short notice. It was here that news arrived that Lieutenant G. Greville had died of his wounds.

6th April The situation was somewhat quieter, and the regiment went on to Vauchelles, which we shared with the 5th Lancers. Captain E. Austin and Lieutenant C. P. Graham rejoined. Everybody hoped to have a week's rest and time to reorganize the squadrons.

7th April A very fine morning, and the Padre came over and we had a church service and Communion. In his sermon the Padre (Rev. Griffiths, C.F.) referred to our recent losses. General Bell-Smyth and Lord Holmpatrick rode over to see how the regiment was getting on. Major A. D. Bell came over in the afternoon to tea; he was staying at Longpré Chateau with General Rankin. This was the last we saw of him, as he was killed in a railway accident the following day on his way down to Rouen.

8th April A wet day. News arrived that the Boche had attacked on the French front south of Compiegne, and we all thought we might find ourselves down there again.

9th April A very dull day. A Lena Ashwell concert party came over from Abbeville in the afternoon, and their show was much appreciated by everybody. All the artistes came to dinner in the chateau afterwards, and then motored back to Abbeville. Lieutenant Dunsby, 2nd-Lieutenant Rea, and 2nd-Lieutenant Underwood arrived as reinforcements. There was a tremendous lot of firing all through the night, which we later discovered to be a Hun attack on the Portuguese.

10th April A fine day. We soon got orders to stand-to at an hour's notice, owing to the Hun attack on the First Army up north. The regiment marched at 3 p.m., via St. Ricquier and La Broye, to Raye, which we all knew pretty well, having been billeted there during the winter 1916–17, and the inhabitants were very glad to see us again.

11th April Remained at Raye, and heard more particulars about the attack on the First Army.

12th April At two hours' notice, marched at 12.30 p.m., via La Broye, Hesdin, and Fruges, to Dennebroecq, getting in late after a very long march.

13th April Still at two hours' notice. Moved off at 1 p.m., and marched, via Therouannes and Wardvecque, to Lynde, and got there about 4 o'clock. There was a bitter wind blowing, and the billeting arrangements took a long time to get settled. This area was pretty well known to us, as we did schemes over it when we were billeted near during 1915.

14th April Stayed at Lynde and heard the most curious and exaggerated reports from refugees, some of whom were no doubt Hun agents. It was a bitterly cold day, and the horses did not look their best. Official information received that Major Bell had been accidentally killed.

15th April The regiment moved off at 7 a.m. to the Bois des Huit Rues, and spent the day there. It was very cold and raw. In the afternoon the C.O. and Squadron Leaders went up to see where we were to go the following day. Returned to Lynde, and received orders to relieve the 16th Lancers at 7 a.m. next day.

16th April Left Lynde at 5.30 a.m. and marched via Morbecque to Papote. On the way saw a small red balloon coming to earth; this was collected and sent to Divisional Headquarters. Spent the whole day there, and were relieved by the Carabiniers in the evening. A French counter-attack started, and there was a great deal of gunning in the direction of Bailleul. Returned to Lynde in the evening.

17th April Stayed at Lynde all day. Again very heavy gunning, and we heard that the French had gained some ground in their attack of the day before. Having lost the Messines Ridge, it appeared that the British troops would be compelled to give up the Ypres Salient. However, the 9th Division won back Wytschaete, but only temporarily. A warning order arrived at 9.45 p.m.

18th April A miserably wet and cold morning. The regiment marched at 11 a.m. to the Flêtre area, and arrived near Caestre. This place was, however, being shelled by the enemy, so we about-turned and went to Hondeghem, and then on to Eecke. There was snow in the evening, and bitterly cold wind. The 5th Lancers were out all night, and had some casualties. We spent the night in farms near Eecke.

19th April A very cold morning, with more snow. All the inhabitants from the farms had cleared off, but they came back this morning to take away their pigs! The 16th Lancers were in a support line near the Mont des Cats. A 6-inch howitzer battery came into our farm, but fortunately did not fire. The regiment remained in billets.

20th April Still very cold and more snow. Had a visit from Brigadier-General Bell-Smyth, who said that the situation appeared to be well in hand, and that he thought the brigade would soon be withdrawn. During the morning a personal reconnaissance was made by the C.O. and the Squadron Commanders, and in the afternoon the regiment went up to relieve the 16th Lancers. The night was a comparatively quiet one.

21st April Intermittent shelling took place all day, but it was distressing to see the Hun shelling the Trappist Monastery on the Mont des Cats. He got several direct hits, one of which went through the roof of the library and did a lot of damage to that part of the building. The 5th Lancers took over from us during the day, and we went back to their billets near Eecke. Some of our horses were lost through shell fire in the afternoon.

22nd April A fine but cold day. We received a list of those who had won distinctions, and these were congratulated by the C.O. Very heavy gunning about 10 p.m. Lieutenant Chichester, who is the intelligence officer, saw a pigeon fly from a loft, and accused the lady of the farm of being a spy. She was very indignant, and nothing more came of the episode.

23rd April A fine day, and the regiment again took over from the 16th Lancers. The night was very noisy, and there was much shelling. "B" Squadron lost one man killed and several horse casualties. Some French "75s" were shooting at top speed, but some were observed by the Hun, and he knocked out most of them and set light to a small French dump.

24th April The brigade was withdrawn from the line, so the regiment came back to their horses, and went off by squadrons to Lynde. Captain Burrell rejoined from leave. Everybody had a well-earned sleep.

During this tour the brigade was under the 9th Corps.

25th April A very fine day. Baths all round, which were very much appreciated. News came through during the day that Villers-Bretonneux and Kemmel Hill had both been lost. The loss of Kemmel Hill came as a great surprise to everybody, as it was considered to be impregnable; but the Hun drenched it with gas to such an extent that the French Division which was holding it was quite unable to stand it. Large working parties of the regiment had worked hard on its defences during the summer of 1916.

26th April Still at Lynde. Several officers went over to see General Rankin at the 4th Brigade Headquarters in the afternoon, and played rounders. Heard we are to move to-morrow, as the area is too crowded.

IN THE GREAT WAR

27th April
28th April
The regiment moved from Lynde at 9 a.m. and marched to Hevringhem; but this area, too, is very cramped. Headquarters and "B" Squadron moved on to Bilques and made more room.

Up to now it has been considered worth while to tabulate each day's work of the regiment from the 21st March. From the maps it will be seen what a large distance was covered. During the period a lot of fighting was done, and casualties were very heavy. Reinforcements in men and horses were continually arriving, and there was hardly any time to reorganize squadrons. The weather, which had favoured the initial Hun attack, gradually got worse, and the cold and snow were a great hardship to both men and horses. However, the results accomplished were most satisfactory, and show what well-trained and well-disciplined troops can do under the most adverse conditions.

29th April to 4th May
The regiment was in billets at Dohem, which on our arrival was full of French troops, but these cleared out. There was news of very heavy fighting up north, but we were holding our own, although the line fluctuated daily. The usual request from Brigade Headquarters arrived asking for the training programme for the following week. The Brigadier inspected the horses, which were wonderful considering what they had been through. Provided the battle goes well, we shall probably move to a more comfortable area near the sea.

4th May
Started for a new area early in the morning. It poured all day, and everybody got wet. Passed near Wismes, which was an old "B" Squadron billet, and arrived at our destination, Beutin and Enoch, about 5 p.m.

6th May to 14th July
During this period the regiment remained in billets at Beutin and Enoch, and after a few days in which to clean up, intensive training started on the 10th. This consisted of section, troop, and squadron training, and, in addition, a certain amount of regimental

THE 4TH (QUEEN'S OWN) HUSSARS

training which was carried out on the sands at Paris Plage; this was always done conjointly with bathing and all forms of sports, dinners being taken out and cooked in the woods. Staff rides, musketry, boxing, football, Hotchkiss gun work, scouting, and intelligence duties were also part of the training. Horse inspections were numerous, and we soon got the horses into such good form that we tied at the second inspection with the Royal Scots Greys and 12th Lancers as being the best in the Division. The Leicester Yeomanry turned out to be very good fellows, and soon adapted themselves to the regular cavalryman's routine.

During the night of the 19th May a lot of hostile aeroplanes came over and bombed Etaples; they did a great deal of damage to the hospitals, and killed many patients and nurses; a hospital train was also hit. On the 20th " C " Squadron football team drew in a match against the 5th Lancers in the semi-final of the Brigade Cup; they won their replay on the 22nd. They then met the 16th Lancers in the final on the 25th, and another draw resulted. In the replay on the 27th " C " Squadron won, and were presented with the cup. On the 29th " C " Squadron was beaten by the 3rd Hussars in the semi-final of the Divisional Cup.

Being situated within a few miles of G.H.Q., we got the latest news every day as to what was going on. On the nights of the 30th and 31st more aeroplanes came over, and again did a good deal of damage to Etaples.

On the 6th June the regiment suffered a very sad loss in the death of Lieutenant W. D. Buddicom, M.C.: he was instructing some of his troop in Hotchkiss gun firing when the gun went off, owing to mechanical defect, and the bullet hit him in the stomach. He was taken to the Duchess of Westminster's hospital, but died the same evening. He was buried on the 8th at Etaples Military Cemetery. In him the regiment lost one of the best officers and a gentleman beloved by all ranks.

Numerous officers and N.C.Os. were sent to courses at the Cavalry Equitation School during this period. It was a very well-run show, and all the students derived much benefit from it. On the 15th June all officers and N.C.Os. went to a gas demonstration. Apart from wearing our own masks, we also had to adjust those for the horses; we then rode through a gas cloud, and it went off with less amusement than was anticipated. Between the 19th and 22nd June the squadrons fired in an A.R.A. competition, and Lieutenant Bailey's troop of " C " Squadron was left in; it was, however, beaten by the 5th Lancers team on the 23rd. The 5th Lancers team eventually won the Corps Competition. On the 22nd June Colonel Campbell, of the Physical Training and Bayonet Fighting School, gave an excellent lecture on fighting, and produced Driscoll to demonstrate : Private Carr, 4th Hussars, gallantly stood up to him, but was beaten on points ! During the evening of the 13th July orders came that the regiment was to move the next morning. It marched via Hesdin to Wamin, as support to the 1st Corps, an attack being thought imminent. On the 16th the march was continued to Anvin. The Corps Commander inspected the regiment *en route*, and was highly pleased with the turn-out and condition of the horses, although it was very hot and dusty.

17th-22nd July The regiment remained in bivouac at Anvin, and we saw a good deal of the tanks. During this time the Commanding Officer and squadron commanders went up to look at the support and reserve trench lines in the 1st Corps area. During this period good news came from the French front, including the recapture of Soissons.

On the 22nd July we marched back to Wamin, and the next day back to our old billets at Beutin and Enoch. Many enemy bombs were dropped during the night of the 24th about Etaples.

THE 4TH (QUEEN'S OWN) HUSSARS

CHAPTER X

23RD JULY—11TH NOVEMBER, 1918

THE VICTORY OFFENSIVE.

23rd July to 1st Aug. During this period training was continued. On the 30th the Commanding Officer and squadron commanders went over to see the billets which we were going to on changing places with the 3rd Hussars. The same evening a very successful boxing competition was held, to which Generals Rankin and Bell-Smyth came. On the 31st " B " Squadron held some excellent sports, to which all the local celebrities came. Private Connal, of the Carabiniers, was very amusing as a clown. During the night Etaples was again bombed; a Hun dropped some bombs at Enoch, and Corporal Latimer of " A " Squadron was wounded, four horses were killed and six wounded. These casualties all occurred in the 3rd Troop of " A " Squadron, then commanded by 2nd-Lieutenant Brennan. It was very bad luck, as this was one of the best troops in the regiment. Fortunately, the bombs fell in a sunken road alongside a field: had they fallen 6 yards farther on, the whole troop, men and horses, would have been wiped out. As it was very hot at the time, all the men were sleeping in the open field. The expression on the faces of the 3rd Hussars billeting party, when they saw the field on the following day, was something to watch. On the 1st August the regiment moved billets to Recques, where everybody was very well off. We remained here until the evening of the 4th August, when, at 9.30 p.m., a move was made via Sorros to Maintenay, where we arrived at 2 a.m. on the 5th.

At 9.15 p.m. marched again via Nampont and Vron to Neuville Hopital, arriving at 2 a.m. on the 6th. The march was a very wet one, and the billeting party, which had gone on, were all fast asleep when the regiment arrived; this caused some very bad language to be used! Marched again at 7 p.m. via Abbeville to Picquigny, where we arrived at 2.30 a.m. on the 7th. It will be observed that all these marches were done by night, so that the Hun should have no indication of the concentration for the 8th August. All horses had to be under cover by dawn, and no movement during the day. The latter was well carried out, as most people went to sleep for a good part of the following day. Few things are so tiring as a succession of night marches. On the 6th the scheme was explained to all officers, and on the 7th it was explained to the men. The regiment moved from Picquigny at 11 p.m. via Dreuil and Amiens. There was a long pause in the latter town, and it was an anxious moment for the higher commands, as so much traffic had to pass through to its jumping-off place. Passing through the town, one could see a good deal of the damage that had been done by the Boche bombardment, especially about the Nord railway-station. At last the column got through, and arrived at Glisy just about dawn, at 4.30 a.m.

8th Aug. The bombardment started at about 4.20 a.m., and it was found that the whole operation was a complete surprise, and the secret had been well kept. This brings out the point that surprise is the secret of a successful operation. The regiment rested for two hours at Glisy, and we received numerous messages of the success of the advance. At about 7 a.m. a move was made via the cavalry track past Cachy to Caix, where we arrived at about 4 p.m. Many dead Germans were seen during the march, and their numerous gun positions had been knocked to pieces. The remains of a Boche tank was passed, which had been knocked out in a tank *versus* tank combat near Villers-Bretonneux earlier in the year. A noticeable feature was that the Boche had not troubled to bury his dead earlier, and some were lying about, almost skeletons. Before the Hun attack in the spring all this ground had been sown, and now the oats and wheat were high and ready for cutting.

After a halt at Caix the regiment was ordered to bivouac for the night in Caix Valley Wood. Truckloads of Boche ammunition were all over the place on light railway trucks, most of which had been captured from the British in the March offensive. The Canadian line was about one and a half miles in front of our bivouac. The amount of material captured was no doubt due to the fact that the Hun was preparing for a great offensive against Amiens later in the year.

9th Aug. This was a very unfortunate day for the regiment, as many casualties in both men and horses were incurred without a shot being fired. At 4 a.m., when it was still dark, "B" Squadron, under Captain Radclyffe, M.C., and "C" Squadron, under Captain Beaman, D.S.O., were sent out to get into touch with the Canadian front line and be prepared to make use of any opportunities of mounted work that might turn up. Headquarters and "A" Squadron, under Captain Evans, M.C., moved up to the east end of Caix village. The infantry advance was timed to commence at 10.30 a.m., but, owing to unforeseen causes, did not actually begin till 1 p.m. The brigade formation was—the 5th Lancers on the right, the 4th Hussars on the left, and the 16th Lancers in support. On the left of the 4th Hussars was the 2nd Brigade, with the 9th Lancers next to the 4th Hussars. During the delay before the attack excellent information was sent back from patrols sent out from "B" and "C" Squadrons, the patrol leaders being Lieutenant France of "B" Squadron and Lieutenant Delius of "C" Squadron. They located positions of hostile machine guns, positions of our infantry posts, and gaps in the wire. It must be remembered that the Canadian infantry had reached the "old Amiens defence line" on the previous evening. Meanwhile

IN THE GREAT WAR

Caix village and East Valley were being freely shelled, and several horses were hit.

A conference of C.Os. was held at Brigade Headquarters at 10 a.m. As the ground over which the 2nd Brigade had to advance was very open, the Brigadier (A. Lawson, C.M.G.) decided to move up the Caix Valley East. This caused a good deal of congestion, especially as tanks and Machine Gun battalions were also using it. A section of R.H.A. was placed at the disposal of the O.C. 4th Hussars. As soon as the attack started at 1 p.m. the hostile infantry could be seen running out from a valley just beyond the Canadian line, and they all made for Warvillers Wood, the first objective for " B " Squadron, which was the advanced guard squadron ; " C " Squadron being brought into support with " A " Squadron. All squadrons were told that no advance would be made until the infantry had reached and gained the line Vrely—Warvillers Wood—Warvillers. As the Huns had cleared from the valley, it was deemed advisable to send the advanced squadron (" B ") into this valley, so that they would be on the east side and clear of the wire of the " old Amiens defence line," and orders were sent to Captain Radclyffe accordingly. Meanwhile Headquarters with " A " and " C " Squadrons moved up towards a gap in the wire. At this time Lieutenant Malcolm was hit, and had to withdraw with a broken elbow-joint. The advanced squadron, very well led by Captain Radclyffe, M.C., gained their valley without loss, except that a pack-horse fell into a trench. Unfortunately, the advanced squadron of the 9th Lancers went beyond the valley up to Vrely, which was still strongly held by the enemy. They suffered heavy casualties, and eventually came back to the valley. This had the natural effect of drawing heavy fire into the valley, which caused heavy losses to the regiment. Up to this there had been but little shelling. 2nd-Lieutenant Job, 4th Hussars, was liaison officer with the advanced squadron of the 9th Lancers. His horse fell, and he, fortunately, fell into a trench. He rejoined the regiment later.

THE 4TH (QUEEN'S OWN) HUSSARS

The C.O., having got the remainder of the regiment up to the gap in the wire, went on to the advanced squadron. About this time the 9th Lancers squadron came into the valley. Shells were soon coming in thick, and Captain Radclyffe, among others, was hit. Lieutenant R. J. V. Falkner then took over command of " B " Squadron. At this moment Sergeant Higgs, the signalling sergeant, rode up to the advanced squadron and reported that all the officers with Headquarters had been knocked out by a single shell, which had landed in the trench in which they were all sitting. On returning to Headquarters the C.O. found that, while examining certain Boche prisoners, a shell pitched in the trench and wounded Major Scott, Captain Christie, Lieutenant Clark, Lieutenant Arkwright, and Lieutenant Dunsby. Captain Evans was the only one to escape untouched. The Boche prisoners were not touched. The O.C. R.H.A. section was also wounded. Major Scott was carried off on a stretcher, the others being able to walk. Another shell landed on the 2nd Brigade Headquarters, killing the signalling officer and wounding the Brigade-Major.

When we eventually reached Warvillers Wood, it was found that there was an admirably placed observation post high up in the trees, from which the Artillery Observation Officer could see practically all down the valley. Captain Evans then became Second-in-Command, and the next item of interest was a flight of Boche machines over us firing off lights. Fortunately, his artillery was then withdrawing and did not fire; but the aeroplanes opened fire, and inflicted some casualties on a Canadian Machine Gun Company which was passing at the time. As we were very congested at the time, " C " Squadron was ordered farther down the valley. Meanwhile Captain Halpin, R.A.M.C., who was attending a wounded man down the valley, was hit, and lost both his legs; he died in hospital two days later. About an hour later 2nd-Lieutenant Underwood, who, with a patrol, was liaison between the 4th Hussars and 5th Lancers, reported that the latter were advancing towards Warvillers. At the same time

2nd-Lieutenant Bailey, who was liaison between the Canadian infantry and "B" Squadron, reported that Vrely was taken, and that the infantry had entered Warvillers Wood. On receipt of these messages the O.C. "B" Squadron (Lieutenant Falkner) pushed on to Warvillers Wood. The C.O. then told Captain Evans to bring on the rest of the regiment to Warvillers Wood. Riding on, the C.O. found the 5th Lancers holding Warvillers, and "B" Squadron holding Warvillers Wood. At this time Sergeant Brunton, 4th Hussars, who was attached to the Intelligence of the 3rd Brigade, searched through Warvillers Chateau, which had been a Hun Divisional Headquarters, and brought out certain papers, giving the whole German plan of battle. These papers proved most useful to the Intelligence. For his action Sergeant Brunton received the Military Medal, as the village was under fire the whole time.

The rest of the regiment now moved up to Warvillers Wood, and everybody got a good view of the huge Hun observation post among the trees, whence the gunfire into Caix Valley had been directed. "B" Squadron pushed through the wood, dismounted, and on arriving on the east side found the Canadian infantry just beyond them. Rouvroy was the next village in the line of advance, but it was necessary to wait until tanks and infantry got a footing. "B" Squadron then mounted and advanced over very open ground to Rouvroy. They could get no farther, so remained in support to the infantry, and supplied them with ammunition. It must be remembered that we had now reached the edge of the old trench system that had been in existence since 1914, and from which the Germans withdrew at the beginning of 1917 as a result of the Somme Battle of 1916. The country therefore became hopeless for cavalry, being a maze of trenches and wire entanglements. Soon afterwards the rest of the regiment proceeded towards Rouvroy, but before getting there came under long-range machine-gun fire from the left flank, which caused some casualties. The order was then given to return to the west side of Warvillers Wood. It then transpired that very little progress had been made on our left, and the 2nd Brigade was not up in the same alignment as Rouvroy. The rest of the brigade also withdrew to the west of Warvillers. Excellent information was sent in from Rouvroy by the O.C. " B " Squadron as to the infantry situation. Also numerous messages had to be sent during the night, and this was gallantly done by Private Pell, who was awarded the Military Medal.

It was now getting late, and orders were issued that the regiment would bivouac for the night where it was, and would be in support to the Canadians. The led horses were accordingly handed over to the No. 3's, and the remainder of the men went to their allotted positions. During the night a hostile aeroplane came over and dropped a bomb right on to Headquarters and the head of " A " Squadron. The result was that Private Flintham, Signaller Greenway, Private Dawson, and Corporal Cheshire were killed, and twelve others were wounded, of whom Private Tull afterwards died of wounds. Also twenty-one horses were killed, and a lot of others broke loose. This will show what damage one bomb can do. Fortunately, only the No. 3's were with the horses at the time, and the cover afforded by the horses no doubt saved further casualties. Private Sharpe had a unique experience, in that all the horses which he was holding were knocked out, but he was untouched. As Captain Halpin, R.A.M.C., had previously been wounded, all the dressings of the wounded men fell on Lance-Corporal Fuller, who was the medical orderly. He worked splendidly, and was awarded the Military Medal for his fine efforts. The rest of the night was very quiet. A point to be brought out here is that the element of surprise, which was so successful the first day, could not be expected to recur the next day ; also the ground now was very unsuitable for mounted work.

10th Aug. About 7 a.m. a squadron of the Royal Dragoons came up to take over from " B " Squadron at Rouvroy. After collecting some forage and rations, the regiment withdrew to Caix Valley, expecting to be there for at least a day. During the morning numerous horses which had been wounded the night before had to be destroyed, including Captain Evans' " William," which had been through the whole war. At 1 p.m. the order came to saddle up and move again towards Warvillers Wood. This was mere optimism on the part of Higher Commands. The regiment hung about in this area till dusk, and was then ordered to bivouac near in the open. There was no water available for the horses. *Experientia docet*, so all ranks were ordered to dig a small hole in the ground as shelter, and each horse was picqueted on its own peg. During the night bombs were again dropped, and Lieutenant Norman's troop ceased to exist, twenty-two horses being killed, and eleven more had to be evacuated next day. There were no casualties among the men.

11th Aug. The C.O. inspected the damage. The bombs had fallen exactly midway between Lieutenant Norman's troop and a long row of Canadian heavy draught horses, tied to wagons, and packed like sardines. None of the latter were touched! During the day the regiment remained where it was, and numerous air combats were seen. Finally, at 4.15 p.m., orders came to withdraw to Caix Valley West, and everybody got settled in just before dark. The bivouac was very dirty, with much smelly meat and barrels of jam lying about, just as they had been left by the Boche on the 8th. Here we heard that on the night of the 8th–9th Interpreter Lépine had been hit. The other two divisions were withdrawn to the Amiens area.

12th Aug. This day was very hot, and most of the remains of the regiment were engaged in burying horses—a very necessary but thankless task!

13th Aug. Lieutenant Ash went off to the Corps School, and there did not appear much prospect of cavalry work. In the evening eight officers, 42 other ranks, and 140 horses, under Lieutenant Sykes, arrived to replace casualties. The rumour at Abbeville had been that the regiment had been annihilated on the 9th!

THE 4TH (QUEEN'S OWN) HUSSARS

14th Aug. General Bell-Smyth, Lord Holmpatrick, and the C.O. motored out to Moreuil Wood, where the regiment had had such a bad time in March and April. A tour was made through Moreuil Wood, where the Boche had advanced on the 1st April. The trenches which the 8th Division had dug after relieving us on the night of the 30th–31st March were still there, and the country was not much changed, except that the French had done a lot of shelling before they advanced on the 8th August. The Senegalese had attacked over this area, but had not had many casualties. Among the immense amount of stuff left by the Boche the number of Lewis guns and British ammunition which he had captured during his March offensive, and used against us, was very noticeable. One could now really realize what the loss of Windmill Hill would have meant on the 31st March, and how the defence of it by the 3rd Cavalry Brigade had helped to such a large extent to save Amiens. Colonel Darley's grave was visited, but a wall had been blown on top of it, so the bricks were removed and another cross put up to mark the spot. On returning to Caix Valley we were warned that we should move in the morning. Every night bombs were dropped, but we escaped any further casualties.

15th Aug. The regiment moved from Caix Valley at 8.15 a.m., and marched back by the track we had used on the 8th August past Glisy and Amiens to Argoeuves, where we billeted. Captain Radclyffe was reported to have died of wounds—fortunately not true.

16th Aug. Lieutenant R. J. V. Falkner, M.C., went on leave from here. The regiment moved at 10.15 p.m., and arrived at Halloy at 2.15 a.m. next day. This was more to avoid traffic than anything else.

17th Aug. Spent the day at Halloy, and restarted again at 10.45 p.m. for Willencourt, near Auxi-le-Chateau, which was reached at about 3.30 a.m. The billets here were very good, and " B " Echelon joined us on the 18th.

IN THE GREAT WAR

The casualties from the 8th to the 17th August, inclusive, were nine officers and forty-five other ranks.

18th-20th Aug. Remained at Willencourt. Cavalry Corps were at Auxi-le-Chateau. Lieutenant Dunsby, who had been knocked out on the 9th, rejoined on the 19th, none the worse. At 5 p.m. on the 20th the regiment was put at two hours' notice. Meanwhile the battle was going on well.

21st Aug. Heard in the morning that our attack had started in front of Arras; this led up to the breaking of the Hindenburg Line. The regiment marched at 8.30 p.m. via Lucheux to Coullemont, which was reached at about 3 a.m. This night march was partly for secrecy and partly to avoid the heat of the day, which at this time was very severe.

22nd-23rd Aug. Remained at Coullemont, and heard that our attack was going well. Sudden orders to move at 4.30 p.m., and marched to Ransart, but, finding no water there, went on to Riviere, arriving in the dark.

24th Aug. Moved on at 5.30 a.m. to Ayette, where there was a halt for an hour or so. At 8 a.m. hurried orders arrived, and off the regiment went towards St. Leger in support to the Guards. "A" Squadron, under Captain Cardwell, was advanced squadron, and Lieutenant Brennan did some very good work, as also did all the 3rd Troop of "A" Squadron. They had a rotten time, as there was a lot of gas about, which caused several casualties. There were nine casualties during the day, all in "A" Squadron. The Guards could not advance against the hostile machine-gun fire, which came from the high ground about Croisille, so the regiment had to stay out in the open during the whole day; there was no cover available, and although enemy aeroplanes were flying about, we were not shelled. A patrol of "C" Squadron, under Lieutenant Morrison, did good work in keeping liaison with the division on the left; and Lieutenant Humphreys, of "B" Squadron, with his patrol sent in valuable information as to the attack on the right. This latter attack was carried out in the afternoon by the 99th Infantry Brigade with the assistance of tanks against Mory Copse. A splendid view was got of the artillery barrage, and one could easily see the Germans " legging it " as the tanks advanced, and our infantry advancing behind. At the top of the hill where the copse was a battery of 77's was in action, and as the tanks reached the crest they were knocked out one by one; but our infantry reached and occupied the copse, which was a very important tactical feature. A squadron of the 16th Lancers tried to co-operate, but they soon found the wire too much for them, so returned to the valley near Ervillers. At 5.30 p.m. orders were received to withdraw. The regiment watered at some troughs which had been put up by the R.Es. that day, and went into bivouac at Monchy-au-Bois, where we found rations and forage. " A " Squadron did not appear till the next day, owing to blocks in the traffic and darkness. The whole area was very heavily bombed during the night, and Major Evans had a lucky escape; he was riding down a sunken road when a bomb dropped on the top of the bank, and fragments flew in all directions just above his head.

On the 25th August the regiment marched back to Coullemont, starting at 6.30 a.m. Some reinforcements came up during the day, and Captain Christie returned; he was hit on the 9th, and during his absence Lieutenant Delius did the work of Adjutant.

25th Aug. to 5th Sept. The regiment remained at Coullemont, and training was carried on, especially with horses, many of the remounts being very green. On the 27th the " B " Echelon rejoined, it having been left at Willencourt.

There was a perfect plague of wasps, and many nests were destroyed. Every night a large number of our aeroplanes, lit up, went over to bomb the Hun back areas. On the 30th Lieutenants Howe, Lunan, and Marshall arrived as reinforcements. On the 31st news came through that the 2nd Australian Division had captured Mt. St. Quintin, near Peronne.

IN THE GREAT WAR

On the 6th September the regiment went to the First Army area, and marched at 10.15 a.m. to Gouves, which was a new area for everybody. On the 7th Lieutenant Nicole, of the Royal Air Force, called. He was a Hotchkiss gun corporal in " A " Squadron, and left the regiment at Raye to get his commission. It was now decided that one regiment from the 3rd Brigade should be sent to each of the corps in the First Army. The result of the draw was—the 4th Hussars to the 8th Corps, the 5th Lancers to the 1st Corps, and the 16th Lancers to the 22nd Corps. On the 9th the Brigadier and all the Regimental Commanders motored round to visit all the Corps Headquarters and collect any maps they could.

On the 10th September the regiment marched to Divion, where everybody got good billets, and the horses were in a good stable.

10th-27th Sept.
The regiment remained at Divion. The weather for the first few days was very wet and blowy. Trumpet-Major Hewett rejoined on the 13th, having been away on General Gough's staff since the beginning of the war. On the 12th the C.O. and Squadron Commanders motored to the 8th Division (General Heneker's), and then went on to the Vimy Ridge, where a splendid view was obtainable to Douai. On the 14th another visit was paid to the 20th Division (General Carey's) and the 24th Division (General Daly's). These were the divisions in the 8th Corps, to which the regiment was attached. Squadron and regimental training took place during this period, special attention being paid to divisional cavalry work. On the evening of the 20th an excellent concert was given by the entertainment troupe of the 1st Division. On the 23rd all squadrons had a unique shoot at moving tanks on the 1st Army Tank Artillery School. This was a great success. On the 25th we were all delighted to see Major Murray-Baillie, who stayed a few days with the regiment. He was the only old 4th Hussars officer to visit the regiment. That evening another excellent concert was given by the 24th Division, and was greatly appreciated. On the afternoon of the 26th the band of the 2nd Life Guards played a selection

in our lines. During this time good news came in from all the theatres of operations. On the 28th the warning order was received in the afternoon, and the regiment marched at 8 p.m. via Bajus, Haute-Auvesnes, and Warlus to Weilly, arriving at about 2.30 a.m. after a cold but fine march. Horses were in the open here, and the men in Adrian huts. On the 29th, after a quiet morning, it started to rain very heavily at 6 p.m. and continued till 10.30 p.m. As no orders for a move had arrived, everybody expected another peaceful night's sleep. However, at 10.45 p.m. orders came in, and the march was resumed at 12 midnight, via Croiselles and Queant, to Inchy Lock, where we arrived at 6 a.m. The march was all through devastated area, and it was very cold.

30th Sept. to 17th Oct. Remained in bivouac near Inchy Lock. When it became light on the 30th it was found that the field allotted to the regiment was a mass of recent shell-holes. This was due to the fact that the Canadians had attacked the canal the day previous, and had pushed on through Bourlon Wood—a wonderful advance for one day. Everybody got busy and dug themselves in. Fortunately, there was a large Boche engineer dump quite close, and we got a lot of material from it. The result was when the regiment left there was a regular underground town: even some of the horses had underground stables. Although there was a lot of bombing in the area, we suffered no casualties except one horse wounded. The Canal du Nord was very interesting, as one could see exactly how the Boche had held it, and all his bombs, machine guns, and ammunition were just as he left them when he fled from this part of the canal. The Canadians did not make a direct attack on it here, but turned it by forcing a crossing near Moeuvres. This part of the line had been held by a German Cavalry Division, and most of the stuff they left behind was almost brand new.

All lights and fires had to be out at dusk owing to hostile bombing, and the well-known shout of " Put that —— light out !"

was again to be heard. A number of officers and other ranks took the opportunity of visiting Bourlon Wood and seeing the pits where the dismounted company of the regiment had such a bad time in November, 1917. Lieutenant Fisher-Smith's grave was quite intact. A wonderful view of Cambrai could be got from the wood, and the Canadians were close up to it. Fires lit by the Boche could be seen burning in the centre of the town. Moeuvres was also within easy walking distance, and the whole countryside was full of interest. News continued to be good. There was a 9-inch gun of ours near our bivouac, and it made a lot of noise; it was firing towards Denain, across the Scarpe Canal. On the 8th October the regiment was put at four hours' notice, and later in the day at two hours' notice. The attack of the Third and Fourth Armies was going well, and numerous reports of the 1st and 3rd Divisions getting through were frequent. On the 10th October a good view was obtained of a Boche machine which shot down two of our observation balloons; it was all over in about fifteen seconds. All our observers came down safely in their parachutes. Heard that the Second Army had attacked and taken Roulers. On the evening of the 17th orders came in that the regiment was to move the next day and join the 8th Corps, which was now advancing on Douai.

18th Oct. A very thick morning. Marched at 9.30 a.m., via Dury and Lecluse, to Esquershin, arriving about 2.30 p.m.
The billeting party lost its way, and only arrived at the same time as the regiment. The march was made unnecessarily long by the Staff not notifying us that the bridge at Etang was not repaired. The echelons arrived at 6 p.m. The village had been heavily shelled the previous day, but the Hun had withdrawn his guns by the time we got there.

19th Oct. In the early morning "B" Squadron, under Lieutenant Hayhurst-France, M.C., and "C" Squadron, under Lieutenant Sykes, went off to co-operate with their respective divisions—*i.e.*, "B" Squadron with the 12th

THE 4TH (QUEEN'S OWN) HUSSARS

Division (General Higginson), and " C " Squadron with the 8th Division (General Heneker). Headquarters and " A " Squadron moved on to Noyelle Godault. All horses got into stables, and men were all in beds. The village was surrounded with small holdings, which were full of vegetables of every kind; these were very much appreciated during our stay.

20th-23rd Oct. Remained at Noyelle Godault. The whole district was full of delay action mines, and during the evening of the 21st one went up in the local brewery at the end of the village. There were some horses in the stable, but no harm was done, although the stable door was blown in. There was a strong smell of gas in several of the houses, and these were avoided. On the 21st news came in that Lieutenant Morrison and his servant, Private Bishop, had been killed the previous day; also that " B " Squadron had had some casualties, including 2nd-Lieutenant Marshall, who was wounded. On the 23rd the 52nd (Lowland) Division arrived, so the C.O. took Captain Cardwell, who was commanding " A " Squadron, to see the G.O.C. (General Mitchell), as " A " Squadron was to work with them when they went into the line. All the mines in this area had been destroyed by the Hun, and there were no inhabitants in any of the villages.

24th Oct. The work done by the squadrons is shown in the reports by the Squadron Commanders (Appendix C).
A start was made at 8 a.m., and the regiment, less " B " and " C " Squadrons, marched via Auby—Flines—Orchies to Rue d'Orchies. As we proceeded, we gradually came to villages full of inhabitants. The Hun had taken all their cattle and horses, and left them only a few sheep and rabbits. " B " and " C " Squadrons were quite close to the billet, which was an excellent one. Meanwhile the 8th Corps Headquarters moved up to Orchies. Here we heard Valenciennes had been taken by the Canadians.

IN THE GREAT WAR

25th Oct. to 9th Nov. Both "B" and "C" Squadrons came in reserve again. On the 26th General Bell-Smyth called with maps, and explained what the 1st and 3rd Cavalry Divisions had done on the 8th, 9th and 10th near Le Cateau.

On the 8th November "A" Squadron went up to the 52nd Division, who were in the line. The work done is given in Captain Cardwell's report (Appendix C).

10th Nov. The regiment, less "A" Squadron, marched at 7 a.m. via St. Amand (which was previously taken by Lieutenant Howe's troop of "C" Squadron) to Bernissart, which was just over the frontier into Belgium. On arrival "C" Squadron received orders to rejoin the 8th Division, and "B" Squadron to relieve "A" Squadron. In this area every bridge and culvert had been destroyed by the Hun.

11th Nov. "C" Squadron moved off at 6 a.m., and "B" Squadron at 10 a.m. As all three squadrons were now detached, Headquarters moved on to Villerot and picked up "A" Squadron. A message had been previously received to say that all fighting was to cease at 11 a.m., and that the Boche had signed the Allied armistice terms. At 11 a.m. all firing ceased.

And so ended the Great War that had been going on for four years and three months. The way in which the troops in the front line accepted the armistice at 11 a.m. on the 11th November was rather a curious one. There was nothing in the way of cheering or any demonstration; men merely dismounted and sat on the side of the road, and, pulling out a cigarette, proceeded to light it, and the only remark was: "Well, thank God that's over!" One had got so accustomed to war and all its horrors that it was at first hard to realize that it was really at an end. The armistice terms were soon made known, and all ranks knew that the next move would be to march forward into Germany. During the war 115 officers had served with the regiment, of whom 20 were killed and 25 wounded.

THE 4TH (QUEEN'S OWN) HUSSARS

It is no exaggeration to say that at this time the regiment was in very good fighting form. All ranks had their tails thoroughly well up, and there was that feeling of supremacy over the enemy which permeated all through. The previous training periods had proved of great value, and each squadron had had its own show with whichever division it was attached to.

The report from General Heneker, who commanded the 8th Division (Appendix C), shows how much the infantry appreciated the work of the cavalry. The regiment felt very proud when it received the letters from General Hunter-Weston, General Kavanagh, and General Pitman (Appendix D), and all ranks knew that their excellent work and sacrifices had been appreciated. No regiment had done better work during the closing days of the struggle. The names of all ranks are given who served continuously with the regiment since August, 1914. (Appendix I.)

The last casualty in killed that the regiment suffered was No. 82556 Private J. J. Quinn, of " A " Squadron, on the 9th November, 1918. He was one of the advanced points when shot dead by machine-gun fire. He was buried the following day by the civilians at Villerot Cemetery, and the grave was a mass of flowers. This will show the feeling which existed between the British and Belgians at this period. The address given at the grave is as follows :—

" La grande faucheuse des champs de bataille ne s'arrête jamais sur son chemin pour y recueillir les gerbes ensanglantées qu'elle y a laissées. C'est à nous de les recueillir et de les entourer de nos soins les plus chaleureux.

" A cet effet, chers alliés belges tous, nous nous sommes empressés autour de l'honorable dépouille de ce valeureux soldat anglais catholique, mort au champ d'honneur en coopérant à la délivrance de votre gentil et hospitalier petit village de Villerot. C'est déjà une marque de reconnaissance d'assister en si grand nombre aux funérailles de notre vaillant allié anglais, mais notre reconnaissance ne doit pas là se borner. 'Per vias rectas,' par le droit chemin, telle fut toujours la haute et fière devise de votre héroïque et sublime Belgique, mais telle est aussi la devise de l'Angleterre et de ses nobles alliés.

"En d'autres termes plus explicites, nous marchons au combat pour la civilisation, le droit et la justice contre la barbarie et la savaugerie allemandes. N'oubliez donc jamais que les fils de l'Angleterre et les alliés tous hommes d'honneur contribuent à chasser de la paisible et innocente Belgique les barbares d'Outre-Rhin et pour vous inculquer une éternelle reconnaissance permettez moi, chers alliés belges, d'établir une comparaison entre l'attitude de ce valeureux soldat anglais et celle de l'ignoble allemand.

"L'un est venu s'immoler sur une terre étrangère pour délivrer celle-ci du joug et de l'appression du militarisme prussien, l'autre, l'allemand, y est venu pour voler, piller, incendier ; son œuvre est celle d'un brigand de grand chemin, d'un vandale. L'un est chéri, l'autre détesté.

"Aussi est ce avec une profonde douleur et un regret justifié que nous avons appris la mort cruelle de ce brave soldat anglais qui repose maintenant loin des siens.

"C'est donc à vous, ô braves et nobles belges qu'incombe le soin et le devoir de fleurir sa tombe chaque année. Oh, je vous en prie, au nom de ceux qui nous sont chers, venez souvent déposer sur cette tombe une gerbe de fleurs. Aussi est-ce le moment de rappeler les paroles d'un grand poète français :

"Ceux qui pieusement sont morts pour la patrie
Ont droit qu'à leur cercueil la foule vienne et prie
Entre les plus beaux noms, leur nom est le plus beau
Toute gloire près d'eux passe et tombe éphémère
Et comme ferait une mère
La voix d'un peuple entier les berce en leur tombeau.

"Et toi, vaillant soldat anglais, repose bien en paix dans les plis de ton cher drapeau."

THE 4TH (QUEEN'S OWN) HUSSARS

[TRANSLATION.]

"The great mowing-machine of the battlefields does not stop in its course to gather up the bleeding sheaves it has left there. It is for us to gather them up and surround them with our greatest respect.

"With this intention, dear Allies, we Belgians have hastened to show honour to the remains of this valiant English Catholic soldier, who died on the field of honour while helping in the deliverance of your charming and hospitable little village of Villerot. It is a mark of gratitude that we are present in such large numbers at the funeral of our valiant English ally, but our gratitude ought not to end there. 'Per vias rectas' ('By the right road')—such was always the high and proud motto of your heroic and sublime Belgium, but such is also the motto of England and her noble Allies.

"In other and more explicit terms, we are fighting for civilization, right, and justice against German barbarity and savageness. Never forget, then, that the sons of England and the Allies, all men of honour, are helping to drive out of peaceful and innocent Belgium the barbarians from the other side of the Rhine; and in order to inculcate in you perpetual gratitude allow me, dear comrades, to establish a comparison between the attitude of this valiant English soldier and that of the ignoble German.

"The one came to sacrifice himself in a foreign land, to deliver it from the oppression of Prussian militarism; the other, the German, came to steal, pillage, burn—his work is that of a highway robber, of a vandal. The one is beloved, the other hated.

"Therefore it is with profound grief and just regret that we have learned of the cruel death of this brave English soldier, who now lies here far from his people.

"It is, then, for us Belgians to take up the duty and task of putting flowers year by year on his grave. I beg of you, in the names of those who are dear to you, to come often to place on this grave a few flowers. It is the moment to recall the words of a great French poet :

> " Those who nobly died for their country
> Deserve that their people should come to their tomb and pray
> Among all noble names their name is most noble ;
> All other glory but theirs passes and fades ephemeral.
> And, as a mother would,
> The voice of a whole nation sings them to sleep in their tomb.

" And you, noble English soldier, rest in peace in the folds of your beloved flag."

The names of the officers who were actually with the regiment on the 11th November are shown in Appendix G. No less than sixty-six other ranks were sent from the regiment for commissions. Their names are given in Appendix J.

In years gone by it was the custom of the regiment to exchange Christmas greetings with the 2nd Chasseurs d'Afrique, and a card was sent, with a covering letter, from the C.O. to the Colonel of the regiment.

The answer was as follows :—

"*Le 7 Janvier*, 1919.

" Mon Colonel,

" C'est au fond du Morvan où je suis en permission de détente de 20 jours que me sont parvenues votre carte et votre lettre de Noël.

" Vous avez fait un beau geste ; je m'y associe de tout cœur et je ne manquerai pas de le porter à la connaissance des officiers, des sous-officiers, des brigadiers et cavaliers du 2me régiment de Chasseurs d'Afrique.

" Il est d'une haute portée morale : nous ne saurions trop louer les prouesses de nos devanciers dans le chemin de la gloire : ils sont nos pères et nous en sommes la race. Voilà pour le passé.

" Pour le présent, votre geste symbolise l'élan de nos cœurs vers un idéal plus élevé et mieux compris du Droit et de la Justice.

"Il est enfin de bon augure pour l'avenir. L'union fait la force et la force assure la paix. Plaise à Dieu que nous ne nous laissions point envahir par les théories fausses du pacifisme et que nous nous rappellins toujours cet adage dicté par la sagesse des Nations : 'Si vis pacem, para bellum.'

"Veuillez agréer, je vous prie, l'assurance de la franche et sincère amitié de votre frère d'armes.

"B. DE CHABANNE,
"*Le Lt.-Colonel Comdt. le 2me Chasseurs d'Afrique.*"

[TRANSLATION.]

7th January, 1919.

"DEAR COLONEL,

"Your card and Christmas letter reached me in the depths of Morvan [Brittany], where I am on twenty days' leave. You have had a happy thought.

"I associate myself with it with all my heart, and I shall not fail to bring it to the notice of the officers, under-officers, corporals and troopers of the 2nd Regiment of Chasseurs d'Afrique.

"It is of high moral import; we cannot praise too highly the prowess of our predecessors in the path of glory; they are our fathers, and we are of the same race. So much for the past.

"For the present, your action symbolizes the movement of our hearts towards a higher and better understood ideal of right and justice.

"It is, finally, of good promise for the future. Unity is strength, and strength assures peace. Please God, we shall not allow ourselves to be invaded by false theories of pacificism, and that we shall always remember the adage prompted by the wisdom of nations : 'If you would have peace prepare for war.'

"Accept, I beg you, the assurance of the frank and sincere friendship of

"Your brother in arms,

"B. DE CHABANNE,
"*Lt.-Colonel, Com. 2nd Chasseurs d'Afrique.*"

APPENDICES

APPENDIX A

ACTION OF 2ND CAVALRY DIVISION (WITH CANADIAN CAVALRY BRIGADE ATTACHED) IN FRONT OF AMIENS, 30TH MARCH–1ST APRIL, 1918

On the night of the 29th–30th March the division was located as under :—

Divisional Headquarters and Divisional Troops	Boves.
3rd Cavalry Brigade	Cottenchy.
4th Cavalry Brigade	Bois de Boves.
5th Cavalry Brigade	Boutillerie and Cagny.
Canadian Cavalry Brigade ...	Guyencourt.

These positions were only reached late at night after a long march from Montdidier, where the division had been holding a line in support of the French.

30th March.—Shortly after 7 a.m. B.G.G.S. 19th Corps rang up on the telephone and said that " enemy reported in large wood north-east of Moreuil on right flank of 20th Division. Cross River Avre at once and move south-east across the Luce and clear up whole situation in wood and secure line as far as Moreuil." As the 3rd and Canadian Cavalry Brigades were closest to the scene of action, General Pitman motored at once to Cottenchy, where he saw General Bell-Smyth, commanding 3rd Cavalry Brigade, at 7.30 a.m., and ordered him to cross the River Avre as rapidly as possible at Le Paraclet, and, moving by the shortest route, to seize the high ground at north-east corner of Moreuil Wood; then, working in conjunction with Canadian Cavalry

Brigade, to restore the situation up to the line of the Moreuil—Dehuin road. The move was to commence as soon as possible, and whichever brigade arrived first at the scene of action was to go straight for the high ground. General Pitman then motored to Guyencourt, saw General Seely, whose brigade was ready to move, and ordered him to cross via Remiencourt and Castel, seize the high ground, and work in conjunction with the 3rd Cavalry Brigade. The situation was so obscure, and time such an important factor, that it was not considered possible to give any further detailed orders. The first brigade to arrive on the scene of action was to act on its own initiative according to circumstances, closely supported by the second. Advanced Divisional Headquarters moved to Gentelles, and the 4th and 5th Cavalry Brigades moved to Bois de Blangy in reserve.

At 9 a.m. the leading regiment of Canadian Cavalry Brigade (the Royal Canadian Dragoons), having crossed the River Avre at Castel without opposition, reached the north-west corner of Moreuil Wood, meeting considerable machine-gun fire from the northern face of the wood.

General Seely issued the following orders :—Advanced guard squadron to clear north-west corner of wood. One squadron to gallop to south-west face of wood. One squadron to gallop round north-east corner and endeavour to join up with second squadron.

At 9.30 a.m. Captain Nordheimer's squadron (R.C.D.) had established themselves in the north-west corner of the wood, though opposed by heavy machine-gun fire. Here they were joined shortly after by Strathcona's Horse.

Captain Newcome's squadron (R.C.D.) penetrated half-way to south-west corner of wood; there they were temporarily checked owing to heavy machine-gun fire from direction of Moreuil. Major Timmis's squadron (R.C.D.) met with very heavy rifle and machine-gun fire, and wheeled to the left, suffering very heavy casualties, and retired.

IN THE GREAT WAR

Lord Strathcona's Horse sent one squadron to reinforce Captain Nordheimer, and remaining two squadrons advanced to the attack, dismounted, on the southern face of the wood. A squadron of Fort Garry Horse attacked the northern face of the wood dismounted. Very fierce fighting ensued in all the northern part of the wood, the enemy showing no signs of desiring to surrender.

In the meantime, at 9.30 a.m., the 3rd Cavalry Brigade, who had crossed the river immediately behind the Canadian Cavalry Brigade and had remained in support, sent a squadron of the 4th Hussars to work down the western edge of the Bois de Moreuil, and to secure the right of the Canadians. Patrols from 5th Lancers attached to the 20th Division about Rifle Wood in C.10–11.

One squadron of Lord Strathcona's Horse, under Lieutenant Flowerdew, was ordered to work round the north-east corner of the wood to support Captain Nordheimer.

Lieutenant Flowerdew's squadron encountered a party of about 300 enemy retiring from the wood in a south-easterly direction, and charged through them twice, killing many with the sword. The squadron then entered the wood about the centre of its eastern face. Here they were joined later by two dismounted squadrons of Lord Strathcona's Horse coming through the wood from the north-west. The remainder of the 4th Hussars (two squadrons) worked along the western slopes of ridge between Moreuil and the wood. The leading squadron of the 4th Hussars (Captain Beaman), having reached track at I.3.b.5.4, got in touch with the Canadians, who had suffered heavy casualties. Verbal orders were received from General Seely to push on along high ground at the point of the wood I.4.a. In endeavouring to do this, they came under accurate close-range machine-gun and field-gun fire, and were forced to retire to track at I.3.b.6.4.

By 11 a.m. the Canadians had established themselves on three sides of the wood, but the centre and southern portions were still full of the enemy.

THE 4TH (QUEEN'S OWN) HUSSARS

At 11.30 a.m. one squadron 16th Lancers was sent to reinforce the 4th Hussars.

At 12.15 p.m. 5th Lancers was sent to get touch with 20th Division, and at 1.30 p.m. were at Hourges. The situation in this neighbourhood being satisfactory, they were withdrawn into Brigade Reserve, leaving a squadron with 20th Division.

At 1 p.m. " A " Squadron, 16th Lancers, was sent to reinforce Canadian line in the wood, and remaining squadron to maintain touch between the Canadians and the 4th Hussars in C.27.d. " A " Squadron proceeded mounted into the wood along track running north and south through centre of wood. On the advanced points approaching C.27.d.8.9. they were fired on with machine guns and rifles by the enemy still in the wood. Squadron retired to C.21.d.3.6. and dismounted, then advanced supported by two machine guns to C.27.d.8.9. Shortly afterwards eighty men of the Warwicks and " C " Squadron, 16th Lancers, came up, and a line was formed with Canadians and 4th Hussars in C.27.c.9.9. and Canadians about C.28.a.3.3.

At 3 p.m. two squadrons 5th Lancers were sent up to reinforce the line in the wood, one of these being made responsible for the left flank. Shortly afterwards the third squadron was used to reinforce.

A general advance all along the line was made at 3 p.m. The whole eastern face of the wood was cleared of the enemy, the line running thence westwards through point I.3.b.9.8. This line was very thin, and about 4.15 p.m. a retirement was made to C.27.d.7.3., where a line was consolidated facing south and east.

Heavy fighting continued all day along the southern and eastern edges of the wood, the enemy making several counter-attacks, accompanied by heavy shelling. Our losses were severe, but the position was maintained, and the cavalry were relieved by the 8th Division at 2.30 a.m. on the 31st. The 3rd Brigade, less 5th Lancers, withdrew to Thiennes, and the Canadian Cavalry Brigade to Bois de Senecat.

1. Returning from Trenches near Hollebeke, October 1914.
2. Church Parade, Le Parc, March 1915.   3 Potijze, May 14th, 1915.
4. Squadron Baths, December 1914.

IN THE GREAT WAR

Action of R.H.A.—" D " Battery came into action about 9.30 a.m. with six guns just east of Windmill. The battery came into action on selected points on far edge of wood on information supplied by Canadian Cavalry Brigade.

Great difficulty in maintaining communication.

About 10.30 a.m. enemy were observed advancing down valley of the Luce, and battery position was moved. On Germans counter-attacking and gaining ground, one section was sent to Hailles to cover retirement of remainder of battery if necessary. By orders of G.O.C. 3rd Cavalry Brigade, one section was sent to position south-west of Castel in order to enfilade German positions east and north-east of Moreuil. Observation was impeded by mist and rain. Towards evening fire was concentrated on eastern edge of wood where enemy had penetrated.

Action of Machine Guns.—At 10 p.m. two guns of 3rd Machine Gun Squadron were sent to support 4th Hussars on western slopes of hill above Moreuil. These two guns had no good targets, but fired on southern corner of wood and on ridge in I.3. central. The remaining two guns went forward into wood with 16th Lancers and took up position on the main north and south track through centre of wood. No good targets fired on. A little grazing fire employed.

Major Laing, commanding the 4th Hussars, sent the following report to Headquarters 3rd Cavalry Brigade regarding the operations of the regiment on the 31st March and the 1st April, 1918 :—

" *Dismounted Action.*—On the 31st March, when the regiment was operating on the south-west side of Cavalry Wood, it was very difficult to keep touch with the Canadian Brigade, who were in the wood, owing to hostile machine-gun fire which was kept up along the western edge of the wood. The difficulty of following the situation in thick woods was well brought out by a squadron which was working dismounted through Cavalry Wood. Progress must necessarily be very slow. Flankers outside the wood at once came under heavy fire. Led horses came under heavy artillery fire from a French battery, which only stopped firing on an officer being sent over to tell them the situation.

"*Mounted Action.*—On the 1st April the regiment rode up to a position on Windmill Hill and dismounted for action. The advance at once stopped as soon as an accurate fire was brought to bear, even at the range of 1,000 yards. Hostile machine guns were spotted, and engaged by automatic weapons, which caused them to move their positions. Patrols sent through Moreuil got into touch with the left of the French, and kept up a continual liaison.

"Our Hotchkiss rifle teams suffered severely, evidently being spotted. More care must be taken in bringing them into action. Every man should be able to work the gun. The guns quickly got choked with mud, which was thrown up by high explosive shells bursting near. The guns want very careful looking after, and should be cleaned and oiled whenever opportunity occurs. Empty strips are liable to be left behind when a position is vacated. All the guns worked well so long as they were kept serviceable, but mud is the danger.

"Communications to the firing line could only be kept up by runners.

"Fire control was strongly exemplified. A burst of fire is absolutely effective in stopping a hostile advance; afterwards a few good shots will stop all movement. The importance of digging in as soon as possible is of the greatest value in saving casualties. The tools are cumbersome, and cannot be used much by day; I think a small entrenching tool would be most beneficial. It is very difficult at times to distinguish the difference between the German and French uniform at any distance, even through glasses."

APPENDIX B

2ND CAVALRY DIVISION: NARRATIVE OF OPERATIONS, 1ST APRIL, 1918

AT 9.20 p.m. on the 31st March the following order was received from 19th Corps (G. 321) :—

" 2nd Cavalry Division will establish to-morrow morning the line C.15. central—C.16. central—Point 104 in C.11.d.—thence north to Hangard, exclusive. Arrangements have been made for artillery preparation on the area involved and neighbouring areas up to 5.38 a.m."

This hour was subsequently altered to 9 a.m., at the request of General Pitman, so that Commanders should have a chance of reconnoitring the ground by daylight.

A conference of Brigadiers was held at Advanced Divisional Headquarters, Gentelles, during the night, when the proposed operations were considered and orders issued.

German Dispositions.—On the morning of the 1st April the German dispositions appeared to have been as follows :—

The Domart—Beaucourt road formed the boundary between the 208th and 19th Divisions, with 208th Division on right (north) and 19th Division on left (south). The 185th Infantry Regiment was the left regiment of 208th Division.

The 74th Infantry Regiment, of 19th Division, held the line southwards from the Domart—Beaucourt road, inclusive. The wood in C.10 and 11 was held by the 2nd and 3rd Battalions, with 1st Battalion in reserve. The other two regiments of the 19th Division were stated to be present, but were not in the line.

THE 4TH (QUEEN'S OWN) HUSSARS

South of the 74th Infantry Regiment, prisoners believed, was the 237th Reserve Infantry Regiment, of the 199th Division.

Plan.—As the enemy had excellent observation over the slopes running from Gentelles to the River Luce, G.O.C. decided to assemble the division before dawn (less 3rd Cavalry Brigade, Carabiniers, and one squadron 3rd Hussars, who were already holding line) under cover, in the low ground between Hourges and Thiennes; also to get "D," "E," and "J" Batteries R.H.A. into position before dawn, from which they could cover the attack. It was decided to attack the wood from the north and north-west under cover of an artillery and machine-gun barrage.

Orders for Attack.—The attack was ordered to take place in three waves—

First Wave: 4th Cavalry Brigade (less troops holding line—*i.e.*, Carabiniers and one squadron 3rd Hussars) to seize objectives—*i.e.*, T-roads at north-east corner of wood to road at C.5. central.

Second Wave: One regiment 5th Cavalry Brigade (20th Hussars) to seize north-east edge of wood along main road, where they were to establish themselves in the wood, forming strong points at each corner of wood.

Third Wave: Canadian Cavalry Brigade to pass through second wave and establish themselves round perimeter of wood, sending standing patrols to Point 104 if possible.

3rd Cavalry Brigade.—Owing to the tactical situation, none of the 3rd Cavalry Brigade who were holding the line could be withdrawn, and every available man had already been brought up to strengthen the line, which was very weak. None of this brigade were therefore available to take part in the actual attack, but protected the right flank of the attack.

The attack was carried through with great dash and gallantry, and reflected the greatest credit on all ranks, especially when it is considered that the division had been in action continuously since the 21st March, during which time they had suffered heavy casualties and had no time for rest or refitting. The enemy machine-gun fire, also artillery and trench mortar fire, directed on the wood all day was very severe, and caused heavy casualties. Between 11.30 a.m. and 3 p.m. the Germans were on several occasions seen massing in large numbers, and were engaged by artillery, machine-gun, and rifle fire. The principal concentration of Germans was seen about 2.30 p.m. The casualties inflicted by the artillery on the enemy were very severe, as good targets were obtained on Germans marching along roads in heavy columns, and were fired on with direct observation, as much as 2,000 rounds being fired by a single battery R.H.A.

The large numbers of German dead in and outside Rifle Wood prove the German losses to have been very heavy, and many more were caused by the fire of " D," " E," and " J " Batteries, R.H.A., assisted by the artillery of the French 29th Division, artillery of the 19th Corps, and by the 19th Siege Battery, which was in action just outside Gentelles, and which on numerous occasions took under their fire places where the enemy were reported to be concentrating. The targets offered to the Horse Batteries by heavy columns moving in the open were taken full advantage of, and very heavy casualties must have been inflicted.

Relief.— The division and attached cavalry regiments were relieved without incident during the night of 1st-2nd, in accordance with G. 508, by the 133rd French Division and 14th (British) Division, when each brigade returned to its horse lines. Relief was not completed until 4.30 a.m.

THE 4TH (QUEEN'S OWN) HUSSARS

APPENDIX C

SUMMARY OF OPERATIONS FROM 18TH OCTOBER TO 11TH NOVEMBER, 1918

"*A*" *Squadron, 4th (Q.O.) Hussars.*

18th October.—Left Inchy for Esquerchin.
19th October.—Left Esquerchin for Noyelle Godault.
24th October.—Left Noyelle-Godault for Rue d'Orchies.
25th October.—Put under orders of 52nd Division as Divisional Cavalry.
26th October.—Lieutenant Booth, with the 2nd Troop and ten other ranks of the 4th Troop, were detailed to report to the 52nd Division Signals as dispatch-riders. This troop was divided as follows:—

With the 155th Brigade	7 other ranks.
With Divisional H.Q. Signals	Remainder of troop.

On the 8th November this troop was divided as follows:—

Divisional Headquarters	4 other ranks.
156th Brigade	4 ,, ,,
157th Brigade	4 ,, ,,

Lieutenant Booth and the remainder of troop rejoined the squadron.

8th November.—Received orders from the 52nd Division to cross the Canal du Jard, and, in co-operation with the 8th Corps Cyclists, establish the line Bonsecours—Le Chene Raoul—Le Cocq.

Liaison was established with the cyclists by Lieutenant Raby and Sergeant Sharp, who crossed the canal on a raft and proceeded direct with the leading company to Bonsecours. At 1530 the bridges had been completed by the Royal Engineers, and the remainder of the squadron then crossed. At 1630 the Squadron Headquarters were established at Le Coran Vert with the cyclists. The Squadron Commander then received orders to send his squadron back to Hergnies for the night.

9th November.—At daybreak the squadron moved forward to Le Coran Vert, and then received orders to move forward with the cyclists to Les Viviers.

At 1100 the squadron received orders to gallop forward and form a bridge-head over the Canal d'Antoing at G.22.8.1. The bridge was partly destroyed, so a dismounted detachment was pushed across the canal as protection to the squadron whilst, with the help of civilians, the bridge was repaired sufficiently to allow single horses being led across. The line was established east of the canal at 1155. Orders were then received to push on (in conjunction with the cyclists on the right flank) through the Bois de Ville and establish the line Le Happart—Couttes—Bruyeres—Coron.

Reconnoitring patrols gained touch with the enemy's rearguard in the wood, and the line was established at the last-mentioned places at 1300.

As our left flank was unprotected, patrols were sent to guard this flank.

At 1420 orders were received to push forward and establish an outpost line for the night on the line Sirault—Villerot, both inclusive. This line was established at 1530, enemy opposition being overcome in both villages.

Squadron's casualties—one other rank killed (H./32556 Private Quinn, J.).

During the night enemy patrols attempted to re-enter Villerot.

THE 4TH (QUEEN'S OWN) HUSSARS

10th November.—At 0730 the outpost line was relieved by cyclist battalion.

Orders were received to push forward through the Bois de Badour at 0930. The squadron advanced and came under shell fire, being under direct observation from guns at Herchies. The squadron continued to advance till it was held up by machine guns at J.1.d.1.4—J.15.a.1.9—I.18.c.9.5. This was reported to the division, and the squadron remained in touch with the enemy. Orders were then received to establish an outpost line, which was taken over by the infantry at dusk, and the squadron returned to billets at Joncquois.

11th November.—Squadron remained in billets at Joncquois till 1200, when it was relieved by " B " Squadron.

" B " Squadron, 4th (Q.O.) Hussars.

18th October.—The squadron moved with the regiment to Esquerchin.

19th October.—The squadron came under the orders of the 12th Division at 0800, and moved to Le Forêt. Orders were received verbally from 12th Division for the squadron less two troops to remain at Le Forêt.

One troop was attached to Signals, 12th Division, and one section from another troop was attached to each of the 35th, 36th, and 37th Brigades.

At 1600 orders were received from 12th Division to pass through Orchies at 0600 the next day, and, moving through the infantry outposts east of that place, to reconnoitre towards the River Escaut and report on state of bridges and location of enemy. The squadron was to cover the front of the division. The direction of the march was slightly altered at 2400 verbally at Divisional Headquarters, and the squadron was notified of the infantry's objective just east of Sameon.

Lieutenant Matthews' and Lieutenant Marshall's patrols, sent out to Lecelles at 1500, did not return that night. They rejoined next day at Rue d'Orchies. Lieutenant Marshall's patrol was knocked out by a shell in Orchies. Lieutenant Matthews' patrol, on passing through the outpost line, was fired at by light machine guns in Rue d'Orchies, and could not get any farther.

20th October.—The squadron moved at 0400, and got into touch with the enemy at 0830, who were holding Sameon and Landas. The infantry were informed, and patrols reported the ground north of Sameon clear of the enemy. Corporal Sharpe made a good reconnaissance of Sameon, and gained information which was of use to the infantry, who quickly drove the enemy out of Sameon and reached their objective, still in touch with the enemy. A patrol to the north-east (Corporal Poole) reached Pont Caillou, where it was held up by machine-gun fire. The bridge over Ruisseau de l'Einon, which was at that time fordable, was destroyed.

The squadron withdrew to Rue d'Orchies at dark in accordance with orders received on the 19th instant.

The roads were *pavé* in good order, but, owing to craters at all crossings and cross-roads, transport could be got up only with great difficulty, and the getting up of rations was greatly delayed.

21st October.—Orders were received from 12th Division. The infantry were to advance to Rumegies on their left, while their right remained in their original position. The same task—reconnoitring—was given the squadron, which passed the infantry outpost line at 0630. The enemy were located along the line of Ruisseau de l'Einon at 0800. The enemy had evidently a line of resistance, and our patrols were unable to advance. Liaison was kept with the corps cyclists on the left of Rue Ruteleux, and posts established there and along the Ruisseau to south of Lecelles. All bridges were blown up by the enemy. Touch was made on the right with the infantry of the 8th Division. Near St. Amand two men of " C " Squadron came up to one of our posts. At 1530 cyclists and infantry occupied Lecelles, and the squadron withdrew to Rue d'Orchies.

THE 4TH (QUEEN'S OWN) HUSSARS

Lieutenant Marshall was wounded by a machine gun, and Corporal Southern's patrol was put out of action on retiring from Rue Bouchard, two horses falling on the *pavé* and one being wounded. All three men ultimately rejoined, two severely injured.

Casualties during the two days were—Lieutenant Marshall wounded; seven other ranks wounded and injured.

The Hotchkiss rifles, under Lieutenants Marshall and Matthews, supported the patrols and fired well, and hits were obtained on one machine gun.

22*nd October.*—Squadron remained at Rue d'Orchies.

23*rd October.*—Squadron moved to Rue de la Place. Captain E. Austin returned from leave.

During the three days Corporals Sharpe, Haynes, and Smith did good work patrolling. Corporals Haynes and Bullen each went back (the former with Lieutenant Matthews) to rescue men whose horses had been hit, and successfully brought them in.

24*th October.*—Remained at Rue de la Place.

25*th October.*—Headquarters, 1st and 3rd Troops came under orders of the regiment.

26*th–28th October.*—Remained at Rue de la Place.

28*th October.*—2nd and 4th Troops rejoined the squadron.

29*th October to 9th November.*—Remained at Rue de la Place.

10*th November.*—Marched to Bernissart.

11*th November.*—Squadron came under orders of 52nd Infantry Division and marched to Jonquois; 1st Troop employed as dispatch riders with Headquarters, 52nd Division, 156th and 157th Infantry Brigades.

IN THE GREAT WAR

"*C*" *Squadron, 4th (Q.O.) Hussars.*

18th October.—The squadron moved with the regiment from Inchy to Esquerchin.

19th November.—The squadron came under the orders of the 8th Infantry Division at 0800. The orders were as follows:—
To reconnoitre the bounds given to the infantry on that date, and report the presence or the absence of the enemy on these bounds.

The infantry were overtaken at their first bound, the Marchiennes—Bouvignies road, which was clear of the enemy.

Lieutenant Delius' troop, which was working on the left, reported the enemy holding the eastern edges of Brillon — Sars-et-Rosieres, the Y-roads in O.1.c., and the railway line in H.36.c.

Lieutenant Morrison's troop, working on the right, which had been held up by a broken bridge at Tilloy, reported later that Brillon and Sars-et-Rosieres were clear of the enemy, and that the enemy had a strong machine-gun post at the cross-roads in O.8.d.

While reconnoitring this last position, Lieutenant Morrison and Private Bishop were killed by a shell, and S.S.-Corporal Rouse was wounded by machine-gun fire and taken prisoner.

No further advance was made on this day.

The squadron withdrew at dusk, according to orders, to 24th Infantry Brigade Headquarters at Cattelet.

20th October.—The squadron moved to Marchiennes.

Owing to the fact that the emergency rations were consumed the previous day, and that the ration wagon with the rations for the 20th did not arrive till 1630 on this date, the squadron was unable to take part in the operations.

The infantry were ordered to make no further advance on this date.

21st October.—The squadron received orders to reconnoitre St. Amand and the canal crossings just east of the town.

THE 4TH (QUEEN'S OWN) HUSSARS

Lieutenant Bailey's troop, working on the right, was held up by machine guns at the cross-roads in O.18.c., at the railway crossing in P.7c., and at bridge in P.13.c. In each case he was unable to advance farther until the machine guns were dislodged by the infantry, who were following close behind.

Lieutenant Howe's troop, working on the left, was held up by machine guns at railway crossing in O.12.b. and at Chau in O.6.d. These machine guns only fired a few shots, and then withdrew. This troop was the first British unit to enter St. Amand.

At 1400 hours a report was sent back that St. Amand was clear of the enemy, that all bridges over the canal were destroyed, and that the crossings were held by machine guns from the farther bank.

The squadron withdrew at dusk to Brillon.

22nd–23rd October.—The squadron remained at Brillon, no bridge fit for horses having been constructed over Canal de la Scarpe.

24th October.—The squadron moved to La Bruyere. A bridge had by this time been constructed over Scarpe Canal, but no bridge over Canal du Jard, which the infantry had reached.

25th–26th October.—Squadron remained at La Bruyere.

27th October.—The squadron moved to Bouvignies, where it came under the orders of the regiment.

28th October to 3rd November.—Squadron remained at Bouvignies.

4th November.—Squadron moved to Beuvry.

5th November.—Squadron moved to La Quenne.

6th–9th November.—Squadron remained at La Quenne.

10th November.—Squadron moved to Bernissart.

11th November.—The squadron came under the orders of the 8th Infantry Division at 0600. The orders were as follows:—To reconnoitre the line Ghlin—J.17. central, the Mons—Jurbise road, and the line Masieres—K.2. central.

IN THE GREAT WAR

The advanced troops overtook the advanced infantry on the line J.29.a—J.4. central.

The line Masieres—K.2. central was reached by 1100. This line was given as the limit of the advance.

A patrol was sent to Casteau, which was reported clear of the enemy.

The squadron withdrew at dusk to Douvrain.

The 8th Divisional report on the work of the squadron during the period is contained in the following :—

Report on work done by " C " Squadron, 4th Hussars, during the period of attachment to 8th Division.

This squadron was very useful during the advance from Bouvignies to the Scarpe east of St. Amand. They were attached to the 8th Division on the 19th October, and were at that time stationed at Esquerchin.

On the 19th October they were given orders to reconnoitre and report the presence or otherwise of the enemy on the lines of the bounds given to the infantry for that day.

To assist them in their work a section of field guns was attached to the squadron. In addition, the Corps cyclists were decentralized to the two leading infantry brigades for the purpose of assisting the cavalry in keeping in touch with the infantry.

They moved forward, reporting at Combined Brigade Headquarters on the way, and got into touch with the enemy east of the Forêt de Marchiennes. Reports were sent back of the presence of the enemy in Sars-et-Rosieres and Brillon, and later of the fact that the enemy had retired. The reconnaissance this day was carried out as far as Rue du Rosier.

On the 20th October no reconnaissance was carried out, as the forage sent forward to them by the regiment did not reach them till late in the afternoon. This day the infantry only made a slight advance, in accordance with 8th Corps orders.

THE 4TH (QUEEN'S OWN) HUSSARS

On the 21st October the cavalry were ordered to reconnoitre St. Amand and to report whether it was held by the enemy; also to report on the crossings of the Scarpe east of St. Amand.

On this day the cavalry had several encounters with the enemy machine guns, and succeeded on two occasions in driving the enemy away without the assistance of the infantry, and on two other occasions engaged and dispersed them by means of the section of Field Artillery attached to them.

The cavalry were the first to enter St. Amand, and reported the town clear at 1500 hours. At the same time reports on the destruction of the bridges over the Scarpe were sent in.

On the 22nd October the cavalry were ordered to get and maintain touch with the 1st Canadian Division in the Forêt de Raismes, and to report the presence or otherwise of the enemy on the Odomez—Bruille Ridge and in the Valley of the Escaut. The cavalry, however, were unable to operate this day owing to the pontoon bridge being twice broken after it had been placed across the Scarpe. They were withdrawn, as the infantry had already carried out the task allotted to the cavalry during the afternoon.

After this date there were no suitable tasks for cavalry, and they were withdrawn into reserve.

During the above period several very useful reports were received from the cavalry as to the state of the roads.

Communications throughout were very good, and close touch was kept with the infantry.

On the 21st October reports were received back from St. Amand to the Squadron Report Centre at intervals of from twenty minutes to half an hour.

The section of guns attached to the squadron were found to be very useful, and in future it has been decided to attach a section to each troop which is operating along a separate road.

The closest co-operation existed between the cavalry and the corps cyclists, and much horseflesh was saved owing to the keenness and energy of the cyclists.

Each evening before dark the cavalry were ordered to withdraw to the vicinity of the leading Brigade Headquarters. This was found to be satisfactory both from point of view of the squadron receiving its rations and forage and also the officer in command obtaining orders for the next day.

It is considered that the infantry obtained considerable benefit from the presence of the cavalry, as the leading infantry were enabled to advance more rapidly and with less fatigue than would have been the case if there had been no screen in front.

(Sgd.) W. C. G. HENEKER, *Major-General,*
Commanding 8th Division.

29*th October*, 1918.

THE 4TH (QUEEN'S OWN) HUSSARS

APPENDIX D

To : G.O.C., 3RD CAVALRY BRIGADE.

I have much pleasure in forwarding the attached communication from G.O.C. 8th Corps and the Cavalry Corps Commander. Please convey to Colonel Laing my appreciation of the excellent work done by his regiment. Kindly return the attached when done with.

T. T. PITMAN, *Major-General,*
Commanding 2nd Cavalry Division.

1st December, 1918.

To : G.O.C., 2ND CAVALRY DIVISION.

The enclosed letter from G.O.C. 8th Corps is forwarded for your information and for transmission to the O.C. 4th Hussars. Will you please congratulate Lieutenant-Colonel Laing from me on the good work his regiment has done, though it is only what I should have expected from them.

C. M. KAVANAGH, *Lieutenant-General,*
Commanding Cavalry Corps.

28th November, 1918.

IN THE GREAT WAR

From: LIEUTENANT-GENERAL SIR AYLMER HUNTER-WESTON,
K.C.B., D.S.O., M.P.,
COMMANDING 8TH ARMY CORPS,
BRITISH ARMIES IN FRANCE.

To: LIEUTENANT-GENERAL SIR C. T. McM. KAVANAGH,
K.C.B., C.V.O., D.S.O.,
COMMANDING THE CAVALRY CORPS,
BRITISH ARMIES IN FRANCE.

HEADQUARTERS, 8TH CORPS.

I shall esteem it a favour if you will transmit to the Officer Commanding the 4th Hussars my appreciation of the excellent work done by his regiment during the time it was attached to the 8th Corps.

Both officers and men displayed initiative, dash, and judgment of a very high order, and the reports sent in by them were of great value to the Commanders concerned.

AYLMER HUNTER-WESTON, *Lieut.-General,*
Commanding 8th Corps.

25th November, 1918.

THE 4TH (QUEEN'S OWN) HUSSARS

APPENDIX E

REPORT ON WIELTJE, 2ND MAY, 1915

2ND CAVALRY DIVISION.

I have the honour to bring to your notice the action of the 4th Hussars and 5th Lancers on the 2nd May.

The 3rd Cavalry Brigade was in dug-outs about 1,300 yards south of the farm in C.22.b. and 300 yards south of the village of Wieltje.

About 5 p.m. a heavy artillery and machine-gun fire was opened by the enemy, who also discharged gas from the vicinity of St. Julien.

I ordered the brigade to put on flannel respirators and be ready to turn out, sending forward a half squadron and machine-gun detachments of each of the three regiments to the redoubts previously dug by the brigade north of Wieltje.

Almost immediately infantry came back towards our dug-outs from the east end of Wieltje village; many of the men were vomiting.

Fearing that our front line had broken, I ordered the 4th Hussars to advance and occupy the trenches vacated by the infantry.

The enemy had evidently observed retiring infantry crossing the Wieltje Ridge, and directed a very heavy artillery fire on it.

Without a moment's delay Major Rankin gave the order to his regiment, " Come on, the 4th Hussars!" and himself led through the thickest shell fire straight into the gas area past the retreating infantry.

Major Rankin was himself twice knocked over by shells, and his adjutant was temporarily stunned; but the regiment advanced through the retreating infantry, the shells, and the gas in the best possible style.

As soon as the regiment had reached the trenches, I ordered Major Rankin to connect with the 4th Cavalry Brigade on his right and the farm in C.22.b. on his left. He replied that he had already done so. I consider that Major Rankin displayed great alacrity, coolness, and initiative, and that the 4th Hussars gave a fine exhibition of nerve, coolness, and discipline. So soon as the 4th Hussars advanced, Lieutenant-Colonel Jardine suggested to me that his regiment should advance through the centre of the village and send out patrols to the north to ascertain if the line had been broken.

I at once ordered him to do this, occupy No. 4 Redoubt, and push in anywhere where there was a gap.

The 5th Lancers advanced in as good form as the 4th Hussars, though not so directly into the gas as the 4th Hussars, but under an equally heavy shell fire.

I consider that Lieutenant-Colonel Jardine showed coolness and soldierly knowledge by the way he handled his regiment, and the reports he sent in to me, and that the 5th Lancers showed great gallantry and discipline in their advance under heavy shell fire and through the gas.

Owing to the fine advance of these two regiments, the 16th Lancers, who I held in reserve, were able to arrest the flight of the gas-stricken infantry.

(Sd.) J. VAUGHAN, *Brigadier-General,*
3rd Cavalry Brigade.

THE 4TH (QUEEN'S OWN) HUSSARS

CAVALRY CORPS.

I am forwarding a report from the G.O.C. 3rd Cavalry Brigade on the action of his brigade on the evening of the 2nd May.

The whole brigade behaved very well under very trying circumstances, and the arrangements made by Brigadier-General Vaughan, in consultation with Brigadier-General Hull, Commanding 10th Brigade, to move up to the support of the infantry were very thorough and well carried out.

The 4th Hussars, under Major Rankin, and the 5th Lancers, under Lieutenant-Colonel Jardine, showed gallantry and good discipline in moving out so promptly to the threatened points, through the retreating infantry and poisonous gasses and under a very heavy shell fire.

(Sd.) C. T. McM. KAVANAGH, *Major-General,*
2nd Cavalry Division.

5th May, 1915.

G.H.Q.

This appears to have been a very good piece of work by the 3rd Cavalry Brigade. I should like to bring to notice the names of Brigadier-General J. Vaughan, Commanding 3rd Cavalry Brigade; Bt. Lieutenant-Colonel J. B. Jardine, Commanding 5th Lancers; Major C. H. Rankin, 7th Hussars, temporarily Commanding 4th Hussars.

(Sd.) E. H. H. ALLENBY, *Lieutenant-General,*
Commanding Cavalry Corps.

6th May, 1915.

IN THE GREAT WAR

APPENDIX F

HONOURS AND AWARDS

Officers.

Name.	*Award.*
T./Lieut.-Gen. Sir G. T. M. Bridges, D.S.O.	K.C.M.G.; C.M.G.; C.B.; three times Mentioned in Despatches; Croix d'Officier de Legion d'Honneur (French); Grand Cordon d'Ordre de Leopold (Belgian); Croix de Guerre (French).
T./Brig.-Gen. P. Howell	C.M.G.; six times Mentioned in Despatches.
T./Brig.-Gen. C. H. Rankin, D.S.O.	C.M.G.; three times Mentioned in Despatches.
T./Brig.-Gen. R. Hoare	C.M.G.; D.S.O.; twice Mentioned in Despatches; Order of St. Stanislaus, 2nd Class, with Swords (Russian).
Lieut.-Col. W. Neilson	D.S.O.; three times Mentioned in Despatches; Order of Karageorge, 4th Class, with Swords (Serbian); Military Cross (Greek).
T./Lieut.-Col. T. W. Pragnell	D.S.O.; three times Mentioned in Despatches.
T./Major F. King	D.S.O.; O.B.E.; twice Mentioned in Despatches.

THE 4TH (QUEEN'S OWN) HUSSARS

Name.	Award.
T./Lieut.-Col. N. O. Laing	D.S.O.; Mentioned in Despatches.
Lieut. A. E. Wass	,, M.C. and bar; Mentioned in Despatches.
Lieut. J. R. V. Sherston	M.C.; Mentioned in Despatches.
Lieut. R. J. V. Falkner	,, ,, ,,
Capt. H. K. D. Evans	,, Twice Mentioned in Despatches.
Lieut. C. B. Ainslie	M.C.; Croix de Guerre (French).
Capt. A. H. Christie	,,
Lieut. R. B. Johnson	,,
Lieut. J. W. S. Morrison	,,
Major H. S. L. Scott	,,
Lieut. W. D. Buddicom	,,
Lieut. V. P. Trew	,,
Capt. M. F. Radclyffe	,, Three times Mentioned in Despatches.
Lieut. H. A. Swain	M.C.; Mentioned in Despatches.
Lieut. A. H. Hayhurst-France	,,
Lieut. W. C. Bailey	,,
Lieut. C. M. Lawrence	,,
Lieut. J. Siddons	,,
Lieut. P. J. Matthews	,,
Lieut. R. W. Howe	,,
Lieut. F. D. Sowerby	,, Croix de Chevalier de Legion d'Honneur (French); Mentioned in Despatches.
Lieut.-Col. C. L. Graham	Order of the Nile, 3rd Class; twice Mentioned in Despatches.
Capt. J. H. Gatacre	Croix de Chevalier de Legion d'Honneur (French).
Lieut. F. A. Sykes	Croix de Guerre (French).
Lieut. F. H. Ash	,, ,, ,,
Capt. A. A. H. Beaman	,, ,, ,,

IN THE GREAT WAR

Name.	Award.
Lieut. G. A. Heinekey	Order of the Nile, 4th Class.
Capt. B. Blood	Mentioned in Despatches.
T./Major Hon. L. H. Cripps	,, ,,
Lieut.-Col. J. E. C. Darley	,, ,,
Lieut. J. T. W. Dunsby	,, ,,
Lieut. K. C. North	Twice Mentioned in Despatches.
T./Major A. F. M. Wilson	,, ,, ,,
Major S. E. W. Thompson	Mentioned in Despatches.
Lieut. C. G. Norman	,, ,,
Lieut. Sir J. H. B. D. Tichborne, Bart.	,, ,,
Capt. G. K. M. Mason	D.S.O.; Mentioned in Despatches.

Other Ranks.

No.	Name.	Award.
8390	Cpl. J. Bowstead	D.C.M. and M.M.
6535	Sgt. W. Stanford	,,
8556	Sgt. W. Siddons	,, and bar; Mentioned in Despatches.
5741	Sgt. A. A. Page	,, Mentioned in Despatches.
4726	S.S.M. C. Hawgood	,,
9360	Sgt. E. Raywood	,,
5390	Sgt. P. Pickles	,,
7028	Pte. G. Ingle	,,
6678	Pte. R. Shaw	,,
6434	Sgt. F. Smith	,,
11352	Sgt. J. Siddons	,, and M.M.; bar to M.M.
4772	Cpl. C. L. Mires	,,
1983	S.S.M. J. T. Brown	,, Italian Bronze Medal.
4923	Sgt. F. G. Holmes	,,
77873	S.S.M. C. Gill	,, Mentioned in Despatches.
45211	R.S.M. T. Pateman	M.M.; twice Mentioned in Despatches.

THE 4TH (QUEEN'S OWN) HUSSARS

No.	Name.	Award.
45242	S.S.M. J. H. Brown	M.M.; Croix de Guerre; Mentioned in Despatches.
7802	Sgt. J. P. Colson	,, Mentioned in Despatches.
10268	L./Cpl. E. Sloane	,, ,, ,,
439	Pte. A. Ewens	,, ,, ,,
10011	Pte. H. Mathews	,,
11285	Sgt. R. Rochford	,, Mentioned in Despatches.
4515	Pte. R. J. Bigg	,,
6508	Sgt. G. F. Higgs	,,
15998	Pte. W. Baldwin	,,
18046	L./Cpl. B. Rowley	,,
10991	L./Cpl. J. Gregory	,,
9008	Pte. W. Neale	,,
14223	Cpl. W. Burgess	,,
8792	Cpl. R. Hamill	,,
1112	Pte. J. Troy	,,
7567	L./Cpl. P. Laker	,,
6527	Pte. E. Swan	,,
6058	L./Cpl. J. Sampson	,,
10084	Sgt. J. Bullen	,,
24167	L./Cpl. D. Evans	,,
8388	Sgt. J. Slater	,, Mentioned in Despatches.
3273	Tptr. H. Mabbett	,,
10167	Pte. C. Rooker	,,
1248	Sgt. A. Chuter	,,
7540	Cpl. S. Law	,,
11256	Pte. W. Alwynne	,,
9402	Pte. R. Reenan	,,
45287	Pte. J. O'Toole	,,
45227	Cpl. C. W. Millest	,,
13343	L./Cpl. E. C. Fuller	,,
10164	L./Cpl. G. H. Sharpe	,,
41210	L./Cpl. W. Haynes	,,

IN THE GREAT WAR

No.	Name.	Award.
255182	Cpl. H. Poole	M.M.
22419	Pte. J. Pell	,,
13289	A./Sgt. F. Brunton	,,
45185	S.Q.M.S. E. Davidge	,,
79113	Sgt. F. Bullen	,,
10028	L./Cpl. H. Bryant	,,
4461	A./Q.M.S. A. H. Beardow	M.S.M.
45183	R.Q.M.S. G. J. Ings	,,
9252	Sgt. J. Brewster	,,
5817	Sgt. F. E. Sharpe	Order of St. George, 4th Class (Russian).
4441	Scotcher, W.	Medaille Militaire (French).
4821	S.S.M. B. W. Dudley	,, ,, ,,
45221	S.S.M. M. Caughlin	Croix de Guerre (Belgian).
45256	Sgt. G. A. Stapley	Croix de Virtute Militaire, 2nd Class (Rumanian).
32284	Pte. R. Croft	Croix de Guerre.
5080	Pte. J. McGregor	,, ,,
21944	L./Cpl. E. Colomb	,, ,,
4441	Sgt. W. Scotcher	Mentioned in Despatches.
1983	S.S.M. J. F. Brown	,, ,, ,,
4462	Sgt. J. Alexander	,, ,, ,, (twice).
5507	Sgt. A. Sparham	,, ,, ,,
3333	L./Sgt. C. S. Scopes	,, ,, ,,
3754	Cpl. P. Lonergan	,, ,, ,,
6627	Cpl. A. E. Robins	,, ,, ,,
1272	Cpl. J. Lynch	,, ,, ,,
8371	Cpl. A. Laver	,, ,, ,,
1252	Cpl. W V. Ashley	,, ,, ,,
4735	Pte. W. Cooper	,, ,, ,,
4411	Pte. F. Clarke	,, ,, ,,
6747	Pte. H. H. Long	,, ,, ,,

THE 4TH (QUEEN'S OWN) HUSSARS

No.	Name.	Award.
4473	Pte. C. W. Turp	Mentioned in Despatches.
6619	Pte. D. T. Newbury	,, ,, ,,
4574	Pte. J. Bennett	,, ,, ,,
1724	Pte. F. Herbert	,, ,, ,,
6035	Pte. C. Pooley	,, ,, ,,
6066	Pte. T. F. Temple	,, ,, ,,
412	Sgt. F. Baker	,, ,, ,,
5486	Pte. A. V. Bradley	,, ,, ,,
10077	Pte. A. H. Hampton	,, ,, ,,
4817	Pte. W. Wright	,, ,, ,,
3718	R.Q.M.S. E. Beardsmore	,, ,, ,,
4821	S.S.M. B. W. Dudley	,, ,, ,,
8777	L./Cpl. F. Underwood	,, ,, ,,
15824	Pte. R. Bearman	,, ,, ,,
4780	Pte. W. Buckler	,, ,, ,,
8142	Pte. C. Jack	,, ,, ,,
5343	Sgt. J. Stoker	,, ,, ,,
8256	Pte. A. May	,, ,, ,,
45183	R.Q.M.S. G. Ings	,, ,, ,,
45167	Q.M.S. L. Bentley	,, ,, ,,
10100	Sgt. F. E. Fletcher	,, ,, ,,
8388	Sgt. J. Slater	Divisional Commander's Card.
4923	Sgt. F. G. Holmes	,, ,, ,,
45283	Cpl. J. Flatley	,, ,, ,,
45159	L./Cpl. W. Mason	,, ,, ,,
14320	Pte. W. Boddy	,, ,, ,,
45210	Pte. J. Bennett	,, ,, ,,
8256	Pte. A. May	,, ,, ,,
6508	Sgt. G. F. Higgs	,, ,, ,,
6258	Pte. A. J. Brent	,, ,, ,,
14223	L./Cpl. W. Burgess	,, ,, ,,
7028	Pte. G. Ingle	,, ,, ,,

IN THE GREAT WAR

No.	Name.	Award.
18046	L./Cpl. B. Rowley	Divisional Commander's Card.
32563	L./Cpl. E. Honeyman	,, ,, ,,
9008	Pte. W. Neale	,, ,, ,,
15998	Pte. W. Baldwin	,, ,, ,,
45299	Sgt. J. Pearce	,, ,, ,,
255182	Cpl. H. Poole	,, ,, ,,
24537	Pte. J. Smith	,, ,, ,,
9252	Sgt. L. Brewster	,, ,, ,,
255207	Sgt. T. Summers	,, ,, ,,
255188	L./Cpl. J. Brown	,, ,, ,,
21944	L./Cpl. E. Colomb	,, ,, ,,
4923	Sgt. F. G. Holmes	,, ,, ,,
7540	Sgt. S. Law	,, ,, ,,
255576	Sgt. A. Goodey	,, ,, ,,
1248	Sgt. A. Chuter	,, ,, ,,
22419	Pte. J. Pell	,, ,, ,,
45244	L./Cpl. T. Smith	,, ,, ,,
13059	L./Cpl. W. Wall	,, ,, ,,
37920	L./Cpl. F. W. Bullen	,, ,, ,,
255785	Cpl. W. Cufflin	,, ,, ,,
45256	Cpl. G. A. Stapley	,, ,, ,,
9219	Cpl. P. Duffley	,, ,, ,,
45276	S.Q.M.S. M. J. Horan	,, ,, ,,
45185	S.Q.M.S. E. J. Davidge	,, ,, ,,
45198	Cpl. J. P. Burke	,, ,, ,,
4356	Pte. H. Barnes	,, ,, ,,
256058	Cpl. H. P. Clifft	,, ,, ,,
45169	Far.-S.S. W. H. Stone	,, ,, ,,
4845	Sgt. J. Pearson	,, ,, ,,
45258	Sgt. J. Thompson	,, ,, ,,
13335	Sgt. H. W. Barker	,, ,, ,,
8148	Pte. S. Bagstaff	,, ,, ,,

THE 4TH (QUEEN'S OWN) HUSSARS

No.	Name.	Award.
2155	Pte. C. Beadle	Divisional Commander's Card.
542	Pte. M. Walshe	,, ,, ,,
419	Pte. P. Finn	,, ,, ,,
22773	Pte. J. A. Wade	,, ,, ,,
45271	Pte. J. H. Morris	,, ,, ,,
2231	Pte. J. A. Hale	,, ,, ,,
115	L./Cpl. J. Doran	,, ,, ,,
9773	Cpl. J. Walsh	,, ,, ,,
45204	Pte. C. W. Webb	,, ,, ,,
45261	Sgt. J. Woodger	,, ,, ,,
45216	Far.-Sgt. F. G. Lewis	,, ,, ,,
8116	S.S.M. A. Cooper	,, ,, ,,

IN THE GREAT WAR

APPENDIX G.

OFFICERS PRESENT WITH THE REGIMENT AT 11 A.M. 11TH NOVEMBER, 1918

Capt. (A./Lieut.-Col.) N. O. Laing.
Capt. (A./Major) H. K. D. Evans, M.C.
Capt. E. Austin.
Capt. R. McK. Cardwell.*
Lieut. A. H. Hayhurst-France, M.C.
Lieut. F. A. Sykes.
Lieut. J. T. W. Dunsby.
Lieut. C. G. Norman.
Lieut. J. D. Delius.
Lieut. C. F. S. Chichester.
Capt. and Qr.Mr. G. Burrell.
2nd-Lieut. H. J. A. Rea.
2nd-Lieut. H. A. Swaine, M.C.†
2nd-Lieut. H. J. Humphries.†
2nd-Lieut. C. Z. M. Booth.†
2nd-Lieut. H. Raby.†
2nd-Lieut. J. S. Standley.†
T./Lieut. P. J. Matthews.
T./Lieut. R. W. Howe.
T./2nd-Lieut. W. C. Bailey, M.C.
T./2nd-Lieut. A. D. J. Brennan.
T./2nd-Lieut. W. Hepburn.
T./Lieut. H. A. Mahood.
T./2nd-Lieut. A. E. Wheeler.
Capt. J. St. A. Titmas.‡

* Sussex Yeomanry, attached. † Leicester Yeomanry, attached.
‡ R.A.M.C. (T.), attached.

THE 4TH (QUEEN'S OWN) HUSSARS

APPENDIX H.

NOMINAL ROLL OF OFFICERS EMBARKING AT DUBLIN, 15TH AUGUST, 1914

In Command ...	Lieut.-Col. I. G. Hogg, D.S.O.
Second-in-Command	Major P. Howell, D.S.O.
"A" *Squadron* ...	Major J. E. Darley.
	Capt. Blakiston Houston, 8th Hussars.
	Capt. J. K. Gatacre, Indian Cavalry.
	Lieut. M. F. Radclyffe.
	Lieut. R. Sherston, Indian Cavalry.
	Lieut. G. Greville.
"B" *Squadron* ...	Capt. T. W. Pragnell.
	Capt. Bindon Blood.
	Lieut. W. A. C. Heyman.
	Lieut. R. J. V. Falkner.
	Lieut. J. H. Sword.
	Lieut. J. R. Lonsdale.
"C" *Squadron* ...	Major H. B. Mockett.
	Capt. H. S. L. Scott.
	Capt. A. Brooke, Indian Cavalry.
	Lieut. Hon. L. H. Cripps.
	Lieut. J. D. Bibby.
	Lieut. B. B. Falkner.
Adjutant	Capt. H. K. D. Evans.
Signalling Officer ...	Lieut. F. King.
Machine Gun Officer	Lieut. K. C. North.
Quartermaster ...	Hon. Lieut. G. Burton.

IN THE GREAT WAR

APPENDIX I.

ROLL OF OFFICERS, WARRANT OFFICERS, NON-COMMISSIONED OFFICERS, AND MEN WHO SERVED CONTINUOUSLY WITH THE REGIMENT BETWEEN 14TH AUGUST, 1914, AND 11TH NOVEMBER, 1918

Officer.

T./Major H. K. D. Evans, M.C.

Warrant Officers.

45211 R.S.M. T. Pateman, M.M.
45183 R.Q.M.S. G. J. Ings.
45189 F.Q.M.S. F. E. Haydon.
45185 S.S.M. E. J. Davidge.

Non-Commissioned Officers and Men.

23	Cpl.	Cahill, G.	90	Pte.	McQuade, T.
419	Pte.	Finn, P.	1209	Tpr.	Pinfold, A. E.
1212	,,	Colmer, W. G.	1213	Pte.	Langley, A. E.
1224	,,	Eyre, W.	1250	,,	Doyle, P.
1594	,,	Walker, H.	1652	,,	Bryans, J.
1795	S.S.	Baker, T. H.	2084	L./Cpl.	Hibbert, J.
2155	Pte.	Beadel, C. S.	2231	Pte.	Hales, J. A.
2412	S.S.	Williams, R. E.	2724	,,	Wood, W. T.
3274	Pte.	Steer, W.	4203	,,	Cowell, C. E.
4227	,,	Robinson, A. J.	4443	Cpl.	Eaton, L.
4923	Sgt.	Holmes, F. G., D.C.M.	5327	Pte.	Jelly, H.

THE 4TH (QUEEN'S OWN) HUSSARS

5386	Pte.	Williams, T.	5400	Pte.	Keene, J. H.
5817	Sgt.	Sharpe, F. E.	6220	,,	Coleman, P.
6258	Cpl.	Brent, A. J.	6508	Sgt.	Higgs, G. F., M.M.
6571	Pte.	Pigden, E.	6742	Pte.	Williams, A. T.
8109	,,	Chilleystone, H. W.	8149	,,	Bagstaff, S.
8230	Cpl.	Harding, W.	8244	,,	Bishop, E. A.
8256	Pte.	May, W. A.	8370	,,	Laver, E.
8377	,,	Brewer, A.	9348	,,	Bennett, H. W.
9800	,,	Donohoe, J.	9801	Sgt.	Newman, T.
9994	,,	Buck, J.	10062	,,	Othen, S. C.
10222	,,	Stringer, E. G.	10238	L./Cpl.	Ackrill, J. W.
10244	Sig.	Fricker, W. H.	11493	Pte.	Cousins, A. S.
45169	F.S.S.	Stone, W. H.	45184	,,	Palfrey, H. H.
45196	S.S.	Bull, G.	45199	,,	Robinson, T. W.
45216	F./Sgt.	Lewis, F. G.	45241	S.S.Cpl.	Freeman, E. G.

IN THE GREAT WAR

APPENDIX J.

ROLL OF WARRANT AND NON-COMMISSIONED OFFICERS AND MEN SERVING WITH THE REGIMENT WHO OBTAINED COMMISSIONS DURING THE WAR

No.	Rank and Name.			Date.
	Cpl.	Bradney	Tank Corps	15/12/15
14221	L./Cpl.	Levin, G. C.	To England	31/12/15
8556	Sgt.	Siddons, W.	10th Bn. Welsh Regt.	12/3/16
26018	Pte.	Spencer, W. S.	11th Bn. Notts and Derby Regt.	30/4/16
4462	Sgt.	Alexander, J.	11th Bn. Northd. Fus.	19/6/16
175	S.S.M.	McLean, T. H.	12th Bn. Northd. Fus.	10/9/16
14248	Pte.	Matthews, G.	10th Bn. Welsh Regt.	11/9/16
16036	L./Cpl.	Danvers, C.	15th Bn. War. Regt.	27/9/16
14311	,,	Gill, R.	To England	22/12/16
13132	,,	Benn, L. W.	6th Bn. K.O.Y.L.I.	25/12/16
21297	,,	Curtiss, J. R.	13th Bn. Rifle Brigade	8/1/17
13346	,,	Jones, R.	To England	30/1/17
14252	,,	Graham, J.	To England	15/2/17
13365	,,	Walpole, E.	13th Bn. Rifle Brigade	19/2/17
15912	,,	Smith, C. H.	2nd Bn. Essex Regt.	19/2/17
22961	Pte.	Rayner, J. C.	To England	21/2/17
4821	S.S.M.	Dudley, B. W.	10th Bn. Worc. Regt.	26/2/17
7802	Sgt.	Colson, J. P.	2nd. Bn. W. Rdg. Regt.	26/2/17
6434	,,	Smith, F.	21st Bn. Middx. Regt.	26/2/17
6086	,,	Dellow, C. F.	10th Bn. Worc. Regt.	26/2/17
5804	,,	Surkett, S.	23rd Bn. Manch. Regt.	26/2/17
6504	,,	Curtis, E. L.	To England	12/4/17

THE 4TH (QUEEN'S OWN) HUSSARS

No.	Rank	and Name.		Date.
6671	Sgt.	Raynham, C.	21st Bn. Middx. Regt.	15/4/17
26364	L./Cpl.	Nicole, J.	To England (R.A.F.)	18/4/17
5821	Sgt.	Harris, L.	To England	7/6/17
206	S.S.M.	McLean, J.	To England	21/6/17
		Bowstead	Norfolk Regt.	15/8/17
6748	Sgt.	Hornby, R.	To England	7/9/17
15917	Pte.	Bysh, G.	To England	11/9/17
22951	L./Cpl.	Davison, F. R.	To England	17/10/17
9630	S.S.M.	Raywood, E.	To Cadet Unit	7/11/17
85860	Pte.	Finley, W. K.	To England	14/11/17
13575	,,	Murrin, J.	To England	27/12/17
16722	L./Cpl.	Hobbs, C.	To England	13/2/18
5382	Sgt.	Anderson, H.	1st Bn. Wilts. Regt.	21/3/18
11351*	Pte.	Cook, F.	To England	25/3/18
6578	Sgt.	York, V. J. W.	1/6th Bn. W. Yorks. R.	10/5/18
11352	,,	Siddons, J.	10th Bn. Cheshire Regt.	10/5/18
8213	,,	Martin, A.	2nd Bn. Suffolk Regt.	10/5/18
7018	,,	Abdy, H. C.	5th Bn. Cam. Highrs.	10/5/18
10085	L./Cpl.	Bean, A. T.	To England	25/5/18
256501†	Cpl.	Burnell, W.	To England	18/6/18
11898	L./Cpl.	Ellis, A.	To England	28/7/18
255549†	,,	Wacks, P. J.	To England	29/7/18
24137	Sgt.	Widdowson, A.	To England	31/7/18
45299	,,	Pearce, J.	To Cadet School	11/8/18
1214	L./Sgt.	Wicks, H. W.	To Cadet School	11/8/18
255200†	S.Q.M.S.	Widdowson, G. L.	To England (R.A. Cand.)	25/8/18
255481†	L./Sgt.	Bird, R.	To England	26/8/18
10011	L./Cpl.	Matthews, H.	To England	13/9/18
14342	Cpl.	Jackson, A. J.	To England	7/10/18
10057	,,	Luke, C. W.	To England	8/10/18
255352	,,	Hutchingson, A. E.	To England (R.A.F. Candidate)	26/10/18

* Failed in Course.   † Leicester Yeomanry, attached.

IN THE GREAT WAR

APPENDIX K.

NOMINAL ROLL OF OFFICERS WHO DIED DURING THE WAR, 4TH AUGUST, 1914, TO 11TH NOVEMBER, 1918

Rank and Name.	Date.	Cause.
Lt.-Col. I. G. Hogg, D.S.O.	2/9/14	Died of wounds.
2nd-Lieut. J. H. Sword	10/9/14	Killed in action.
Capt. J. K. Gatacre	12/10/14	,, ,,
Lieut. F. E. Levita	12/10/14	,, ,,
2nd-Lieut. J. R. M. Lonsdale	29/10/14	Died of wounds.
Capt. F. W. Hunt	31/10/14	Killed in action.
Lieut. K. C. North	31/10/14	,, ,,
Lieut. A. F. Schuster	20/11/14	,, ,,
2nd-Lieut. F. D. Sowerby	1/8/16	Died of wounds.
2nd-Lieut. J. Fisher-Smith	28/11/17	Killed in action.
Lieut. D. H. Quinlan	26/3/18	,, ,,
Major J. E. C. Darley	31/3/18	,, ,,
2nd-Lieut. A. F. Myers	31/3/18	,, ,,
Capt. G. G. F. Greville	31/3/18	Died of wounds.
Major A. D. Bell	8/4/18	Railway accident
Lieut. W. D. Buddicom	6/6/18	Died of wounds (accident).
Lieut. J. W. S. Morrison	19/10/18	Killed in action.

THE 4TH (QUEEN'S OWN) HUSSARS

NOMINAL ROLL OF MEN WHO DIED DURING THE WAR, 4TH AUGUST, 1914, TO 11TH NOVEMBER, 1918.

No.	Rank	and Name.	Date.	Cause.
4055	Pte.	Hawkins, E.	24/8/14	Killed in action.
2532	,,	Robinson, G. V.	10/9/14	,, ,,
4823	,,	Marsh, J. T.	13/9/14	Died of wounds.
6713	,,	Read, W.	/9/14	Killed in action.
8793	,,	Bryans, H.	/9/14	,, ,,
8254	L./Cpl.	Smythe, H.	16/10/14	,, ,,
1228	,,	Wakefield, G.	16/10/14	,, ,,
10256	Pte.	Tabner, A.	30/10/14	,, ,,
9998	,,	Wright, G. J.	30/10/14	,, ,,
9777	,,	Byrne, C.	31/10/14	,, ,,
7838	,,	Rewes, C.	31/10/14	,, ,,
2268	,,	Warmock, J.	31/10/14	Died of wounds.
8114	,,	Ewens, F. W. A.	31/10/14	,, ,,
3529	Sgt.	Minton, H.	1/11/14	Killed in action.
3272	Pte.	Dixon, F.	2/11/14	,, ,,
10873	L./Cpl.	Rochford, J.	4/11/14	Died of wounds.
10223	Pte.	Haulkham, L. G. R.	4/11/14	,, ,,
6628	,,	Boird, F. E. G.	5/11/14	Killed in action.
13256	,,	Fagan, J.	5/11/14	,, ,,
5393	,,	Gibson, A.	5/11/14	,, ,,
6624	,,	Green	5/11/14	,, ,,
6619	,,	Newberry, D.	5/11/14	,, ,,
6611	L./Cpl.	Muller, W.	5/11/14	,, ,,
6472	Cpl.	Townroe, J. G.	5/11/14	,, ,,
4753	L./Cpl.	Thompson, J.	5/11/14	,, ,,
4498	Pte.	Conneally, M.	6/11/14	Died of wounds.
1965	,,	Walsh, J.	7/11/14	,, ,,
4527	,,	North, A.	10/11/14	,, ,,
1580	,,	McKeirnian, P.	15/11/14	Died.
4549	,,	Barty, D.	16/12/14	V.D.H.

IN THE GREAT WAR

No.	Rank and Name.	Date.	Cause.
9793	Cpl. Barrett, F. A.	19/12/14	Died of wounds.
3835	Sgt. Peake, W.	16/2/15	Killed in action.
2319	Pte. Chalk, G.	13/3/15	Accident (fractured skull).
10253	,, Chatfield, A.	28/4/15	Killed in action.
9253	,, O'Mahoney, W.	2/5/15	,, ,,
5566	Cpl. Dickens, C. W.	3/5/15	Died of wounds.
9581	Pte. McGarthy, J.	3/5/15	,, ,,
10365	,, Curran, P. J.	5/5/15	,, ,,
12240	,, Rogers, F.	5/5/15	,, ,,
10263	,, McCracken, A.	14/5/15	,, ,,
10227	,, Ivory, T. A.	20/5/15	Killed in action.
4725	,, Walsh, J.	24/5/15	,, ,,
4726	S.S.M. Hawgood, C. B.	24/5/15	,, ,,
6042	Pte. Southwell, W.	25/5/15	,, ,,
11439	,, Walker, J. H. S.	26/5/15	Died of wounds.
9949	,, O'Sullivan, J.	28/5/15	Killed in action.
5706	,, Wilkinson, W.	28/5/15	,, ,,
4223	,, Brown, W.	28/5/15	,, ,,
10357	,, Pagden, H. P.	28/5/15	,, ,,
10002	,, Pluckrose, F. G.	28/5/15	,, ,,
9970	,, Meigh, A.	30/5/15	Died of wounds.
4458	,, Woodstack, R. F.	20/7/15	Killed in action.
10353	,, Robb, R.	23/9/15	Pneumonia.
4234	,, Kerr, R. J.	9/10/15	,,
8371	Sgt. Laver, A.	11/1/16	Died of wounds.
18296	Pte. Cohen, D.	26/1/16	Killed in action.
7834	L./Cpl. Sheridan, A. W.	7/2/16	,, ,,
14323	Pte. Sear, W.	7/2/16	,, ,,
10985	,, Furniss, P.	7/2/16	,, ,,
6335	,, Paviour, F.	7/2/16	,, ,,
9267	,, Nangle, W.	9/2/16	Died of wounds.
13284	Pte. Davies, J.	11/6/16	Killed in action.

THE 4TH (QUEEN'S OWN) HUSSARS

No.	Rank	and Name.	Date.	Cause.
266531	Pte.	Hall, G. S.	23/5/17	Killed in action.
4680	,,	Cummins, R.	5/6/17	,, ,,
14233	,,	Galyer, J.	7/6/17	Died of wounds.
7048	,,	Pugh, W. F.	7/6/17	,, ,,
32500	,,	Rookes, P.	8/7/17	,, ,,
15886	,,	Sims, E. W.	2/12/17	,, ,,
45235	,,	Shaw, S.	11/12/17	Hæmorrhage.
16980	,,	Harmer, W. E.	14/1/18	Killed in action.
45178	,,	Jelliffe, F.	14/1/18	Died of wounds.
8550	,,	Murphy, T. J.	16/1/18	Killed in action.
10723	,,	Whittington, E. D.	9/2/18	Pneumonia.
4550	,,	Marshall, W. G.	23/3/18	Died of wounds.
261352	,,	Wilson, E. D.	23/3/18	Killed in action.
826	,,	McGrath, J.	23/3/18	,, ,,
9196	L./Cpl.	Norton, J. E.	23/3/18	,, ,,
8581	Pte.	O'Callaghan, J.	23/3/18	,, ,,
18161	,,	Terbury, J. H.	23/3/18	,, ,,
13070	,,	Earl, J.	26/3/18	,, ,,
14223	Cpl.	Burgess, W. A.	27/3/18	Died of wounds.
10003	Sgt.	Aedy, T. E.	30/3/18	Killed in action.
10230	Cpl.	Rose, F. E.	30/3/18	,, ,,
18046	L./Cpl.	Rowley, B.	30/3/18	,, ,,
45187	Cpl.	Horton, F.	30/3/18	,, ,,
70	Pte.	Boden, J.	30/3/18	,, ,,
5390	Sgt.	Pickles, P.	31/3/18	,, ,,
45283	L./Sgt.	Flatley, J.	31/3/18	,, ,,
7364	Cpl.	Matthews, W.	31/3/18	,, ,,
35118	Pte.	Hayward, S.	31/3/18	,, ,,
34765	,,	Barker, F. G.	31/3/18	,, ,,
12972	,,	Howard, P.	31/3/18	Died of wounds.
8112	L./Sgt.	Nicholas, W. J.	31/3/18	,, ,,
11256	Pte.	Alwynne, W.	2/4/18	,, ,,
14421	,,	Pugh, A. R. E.	2/4/18	,, ,,

IN THE GREAT WAR

No.	Rank and Name.	Date.	Cause.
1982	Pte. Cairns, A.	6/4/18	Died of wounds.
10991	L./Cpl. Gregory, J.	10/4/18	,, ,,
4544	Pte. Smy, H.	10/4/18	,, ,,
10261	,, Everitt, G.	15/4/18	,, ,,
16024	,, Lord, P.	23/4/18	Killed in action.
31899	,, Williams, J. D.	26/4/18	Died of wounds.
45163	,, McTaggert, D.	23/6/18	Pneumonia.
6614	,, Sorrell, W. J.	18/7/18	Peritonitis.
7025	,, Edwards, A. W.	9/8/18	Killed in action.
45245	,, Wright, W.	9/8/18	,, ,,
4078	,, Flintham, F.	10/8/18	,, ,,
14366	,, Greenway, W.	10/8/18	,, ,,
8365	,, Dawson, F.	10/8/18	,, ,,
6089	,, Tull, W. J.	11/8/18	Died of wounds.
45292	,, Bishop, C. W.	19/10/18	Killed in action.
45177	,, Merrigan, J.	8/11/18	Pneumonia.
32566	,, Quinn, J. J.	9/11/18	Killed in action
16130	,, Riley, M.	15/11/18	Pneumonia.
7544	,, Bigg, A.	3/3/19	Pneumonia.
9370	,, Wood, H.	4/3/19	Influenza.
6877	,, Liebrecht, T. F.	5/19	Died of wounds.

NOMINAL ROLL OF OFFICERS WOUNDED DURING THE WAR, 4TH AUGUST, 1914, TO 11TH NOVEMBER, 1918.

Rank and Name.	Date.
Lieut. J. D. Bibby	28/8/14
2nd-Lieut. B. B. Falkner	28/8/14
2nd-Lieut. G. W. Burrell	14/9/14
2nd-Lieut. J. T. W. Dunsby	12/10/14
Lieut. Hon. L. H. Cripps	2/11/14
Capt. G. K. M. Mason	5/11/14
Lieut. A. Brooke	20/11/14
Capt. A. V. W. Stokes	23/2/15

THE 4TH (QUEEN'S OWN) HUSSARS

Rank and Name.	Date.
Lieut. E. Austin	2/5/15
2nd-Lieut. M. F. Radclyffe, M.C.	2/5/15
T./Lieut. G. C. Gilbert	22/6/17
Capt. H. S. L. Scott, M.C.	29/11/17
Capt. A. A. H. Beaman	14/1/18
Lieut. M. S. Close	23/3/18
2nd-Lieut. C. B. Ainslie	26/3/18
Bt.-Major N. O. Laing, D.S.O.	30/3/18
Lieut. V. P. Trew, M.C.	31/3/18
2nd-Lieut. R. W. Howe	1/4/18
Capt. M. F. Radclyffe, M.C.	9/8/18
Capt. H. S. L. Scott, M.C.	9/8/18
Capt. A. H. Christie	9/8/18
Lieut. R. O. Arkwright	9/8/18
Lieut. P. J. Matthews	9/8/18
Lieut. E. F. P. Clarke	9/8/18
2nd-Lieut. K. J. Malcolm	9/8/18
Lieut. A. M. Marshall	21/10/18

NOMINAL ROLL OF MEN WOUNDED DURING THE WAR, 4TH AUGUST, 1914, TO 11TH NOVEMBER, 1918.

No.	Rank	and Name.	Date.
7557	Pte.	McBride, R.	22/8/14
8763	,,	Morphy, W.	28/8/14
5399	L./Cpl.	McVann, R.	28/8/14
4603	Pte.	Munns, T.	28/8/14
530	,,	Briggs, J.	1/9/14
10262	,,	Orr, J.	2/9/14
9587	,,	McDonald, P.	7/9/14
7018	Cpl.	Abdy, H.	10/9/14
440	Pte.	Amey, L.	10/9/14
9813	,,	Alger, H.	11/9/14

IN THE GREAT WAR

No.	Rank and Name.					Date.
8230	Pte.	Harding, W.	...	...	...	13/9/14
1592	Cpl.	Mount, J.	...	...	...	13/9/14
5378	Pte.	Smith, C.	...	...	...	13/9/14
9806	,,	Arnold, J.	...	...	...	14/9/14
9978	,,	Dillon, A.	...	...	...	14/9/14
2992	R.S.M.	Burrell, G. W.	...	...	...	14/9/14
8886	Pte.	Burden, W.	...	...	...	15/9/14
10100	,,	Fletcher, F.	...	...	...	17/9/14
6383	L./Cpl.	White, J.	...	...	...	26/9/14
1267	,,	Ballancie, T.	...	...	...	1/10/14
3333	L./Sgt.	Scopes, C.	...	...	...	8/10/14
6066	Pte.	Temple, T.	...	...	...	13/10/14
1724	,,	Herbert, F.	...	...	...	13/10/14
4574	,,	Bennell, J.	...	...	...	13/10/14
6068	Sgt.	Dillon, C.	...	...	...	16/10/14
5709	L./Cpl.	Davis, E.	...	...	...	16/10/14
9008	Pte.	Neill, W.	...	...	...	22/10/14
10808	,,	Flanagan, J.	...	...	...	22/10/14
4540	L./Cpl.	McKlevie, W.	...	...	...	25/10/14
10056	Pte.	Hillier, R.	...	...	...	27/10/14
8124	L./Cpl.	Tuppen, F.	...	...	...	27/10/14
8376	Pte.	Studd, W. D.	...	...	...	29/10/14
4802	L./Cpl.	Cox, J.	...	...	...	30/10/14
6596	,,	Myhill, J.	...	...	...	30/10/14
1282	Pte.	O'Neill, M.	...	...	...	30/10/14
1229	,,	Faggetter, S.	...	...	...	30/10/14
9630	Sgt.	Raywood, E.	...	...	...	31/10/14
825	Cpl.	Galvin, J.	...	...	...	31/10/14
9257	L./Cpl.	Lynch, J.	...	...	...	31/10/14
6689	Pte.	Hall, C. J.	...	...	...	31/10/14
8148	,,	Hunt, J.	...	...	...	31/10/14
4253	,,	Keen, W. R.	...	...	...	31/10/14
6576	,,	Crisspin, R.	...	...	...	31/10/14

THE 4TH (QUEEN'S OWN) HUSSARS

No.	Rank and Name.	Date.
6636	Pte. Nolan, P.	31/10/14
10066	,, Peal, S.	31/10/14
10096	,, Rohan, C.	31/10/14
6747	,, Long, H. H.	31/10/14
5486	,, Bradley, A. V.	31/10/14
4461	L./Cpl. Beardow, A.	1/11/14
4473	Pte. Turp, C.	1/11/14
4817	,, Wright, W.	3/11/14
1595	,, Aston, R.	4/11/14
6683	L./Sgt. Byrne, H.	5/11/14
6626	L./Cpl. Beard, H.	5/11/14
5804	,, Surkitt, S.	5/11/14
1232	Pte. Boyd, T.	5/11/14
6151	,, Cooke, A.	5/11/14
13015	,, Keogh, M.	5/11/14
1278	,, Prendergast, J.	5/11/14
9012	,, Russell, H.	5/11/14
4269	,, Barnes, G.	5/11/14
6040	,, Bennett, W.	5/11/14
8142	,, Jack, C.	5/11/14
10263	,, McCracken, A.	5/11/14
4358	,, Marshall, W.	5/11/14
6514	,, Starker, E. J.	5/11/14
14311	,, Gill, R. S.	7/11/14
7049	,, Pascall, E.	7/11/14
4512	,, Price, A.	7/11/14
4875	,, Crawley, W.	7/11/14
412	Sgt. Baker, F.	14/11/14
6416	L./Cpl. Weldon, R.	15/11/14
8585	Pte. Brumhead, E. H.	15/11/14
6535	,, Stanford, W.	15/11/14
9788	,, Duffy, G.	20/11/14
6877	,, Liebrecht, T.	20/11/14

IN THE GREAT WAR

No.	Rank and Name.		Date.
10025	Pte.	Moore, H.	20/11/14
10229	,,	Matthews, P.	21/11/14
5382	Sgt.	Anderson, H.	21/11/14
1344	Pte.	Browne, A.	21/11/14
4562	,,	Clarke, A.	21/11/14
4905	L./Cpl.	Butcher, R.	21/11/14
1287	Sgt.	Seager, E.	21/11/14
1586	Cpl.	Wallington, A.	22/11/14
8366	Pte.	Webb, J.	27/11/14
4186	,,	Stevens, J.	15/2/15
10349	,,	Sharpe, G.	16/2/15
10018	,,	Raybould, C.	16/2/15
8122	,,	Litchfield, F.	16/2/15
9036	,,	King, J.	16/2/15
11439	,,	Walker, J.	18/2/15
6450	L./Cpl.	Ratcliffe, L.	21/2/15
8841	Pte.	Speed, F.	22/2/15
6875	,,	Copus, T.	23/2/15
1237	,,	Donohoe, L.	27/4/15
8122	,,	Litchfield, F.	27/4/15
8569	,,	Freeman, C.	27/4/15
9	,,	Grady, T.	27/4/15
9381	,,	Mitchell, L.	27/4/15
6045	,,	Butler, R.	27/4/15
9774	Cpl.	Kavanagh, M.	27/4/15
5705	L./Cpl.	Coulby, A.	27/4/15
6394	Sgt.	Pugh, W.	28/4/15
6351	L./Cpl.	Dacey, W.	28/4/15
5404	Pte.	Keating, M.	28/4/15
8390	L./Sgt.	Bowstead, J.	30/4/15
337	Cpl.	Thompson, A. E.	2/5/15
6240	Cpl.	Witts, H.	2/5/15
13042	L./Cpl.	Keogh, L.	2/5/15

THE 4TH (QUEEN'S OWN) HUSSARS

No.	Rank	and Name.	Date.
13029	Pte.	McCann, T.	2/5/15
6572	,,	Coulson, D. W.	2/5/15
9800	,,	Donohoe, J.	2/5/15
10058	,,	Coulson, P. R.	2/5/15
4713	,,	Rothery, T.	2/5/15
1232	,,	Boyd, T. J.	2/5/15
7028	,,	Ingle, G.	2/5/15
1225	,,	Dwyer, J.	3/5/15
6655	,,	Bishop	4/5/15
6364	,,	Glaysher, W.	4/5/15
10257	,,	Larnder, E. H.	4/5/15
9402	,,	Reenan, R. W.	4/5/15
7817	L./Cpl.	Bird, P.	4/5/15
6504	Sgt.	Curtiss, E.	8/5/15
10383	Pte.	Kane, W.	14/5/15
8213	Cpl.	Martin, A.	15/5/15
9267	Pte.	Nangle, A.	21/5/15
9015	,,	Browne, J.	21/5/15
9268	,,	Mulrenin, R.	22/5/15
4690	,,	Kelly, J.	24/5/15
4630	,,	Tudbury, T.	24/5/15
5335	,,	Hewitt, L. J.	24/5/15
13892	,,	Sheridan, J.	24/5/15
6321	Tptr.	Hewitt, J.	24/5/15
1223	Cpl.	Stambrey, T.	25/5/15
6621	Pte.	Ayers, H. W.	25/5/15
9813	,,	Alger, H.	25/5/15
10022	,,	Burls, W. H.	25/5/15
10055	,,	Coulson, P.	25/5/15
9970	,,	Meigh, A.	25/5/15
6511	,,	Beckett, F.	26/5/15
1345	,,	Etheridge, P.	26/5/15
11416	,,	Keiper, J.	26/5/15

IN THE GREAT WAR

No.	Rank and Name.		Date.
10057	Pte.	Luke, C. W.	26/5/15
10098	,,	Polfrey, J. H.	26/5/15
10231	,,	Weston, W.	26/5/15
10254	,,	Geraghly, T.	27/5/15
9036	,,	King, J.	27/5/15
70	Cpl.	Boden, J.	27/5/15
10242	Pte.	Songhurst, J.	28/5/15
4780	,,	Buckler, W. H.	28/5/15
7828	,,	Gibson, F.	28/5/15
7050	,,	Weatherstone, E.	28/5/15
9995	,,	Martin, C.	28/5/15
10000	,,	Crow, A.	28/5/15
4764	,,	Toyne, J.	28/5/15
3273	Tptr.	Mabbett, H.	28/5/15
8388	Cpl.	Slater, J.	29/5/15
5336	L./Cpl.	Cook, T.	29/5/15
8143	Pte.	Sinclair, J.	29/5/15
10644	,,	Malone, J.	29/5/15
6553	,,	Tolfrey, H.	29/5/15
5055	,,	Anscombe, A.	29/5/15
4384	,,	Hartley, H.	29/5/15
6527	,,	Swan, E.	29/5/15
9947	,,	Donohoe, J.	29/5/15
18399	,,	Moore, E.	2/6/15
1240	,,	Coffey, B.	4/6/15
14453	,,	Perkins, R.	5/6/15
5372	,,	Docherty, P.	15/7/15
4575	,,	Cameron, N. B.	18/7/15
6640	,,	Ashley, J.	20/7/15
6189	,,	Martin, W.	21/7/15
1252	L./Cpl.	Ashley, W. V.	21/7/15
18296	Pte.	Cohen, D.	4/10/15
7528	,,	Chapman, T.	6/10/15

THE 4TH (QUEEN'S OWN) HUSSARS

No.	Rank	and Name.	Date.
11621	Pte.	Commins, M.	4/1/16
14572	,,	Wood, W.	5/1/16
4235	,,	Sculthorpe, A. E.	5/1/16
14280	,,	Simpson, V.	6/1/16
14196	,,	Weeks, A.	20/1/16
11160	,,	Green, J.	22/1/16
11284	,,	Branch, F. S.	22/1/16
11607	,,	Baker, H.	22/1/16
1235	Sgt.	Coyne, R.	22/1/16
14731	Pte.	Jones, R.	25/1/16
8581	,,	O'Callaghan, J.	26/1/16
4673	,,	McKie, W. C.	26/1/16
10028	,,	Bryant, H.	28/1/16
6604	,,	Hills, F. A.	28/1/16
16011	,,	Webb, A.	30/1/16
5285	,,	Brightman, J.	30/1/16
6614	,,	Sorrell, W.	6/2/16
22788	,,	Meakin, F.	7/2/16
10055	,,	Cowan, C.	7/2/16
6070	Cpl.	Kingswell, C.	7/2/16
11971	Pte.	Hanuy, J. W.	7/2/16
26380	,,	Williams, G.	8/2/16
25041	,,	Henson, J.	8/2/16
14337	,,	Ellis, H.	8/2/16
16678	,,	O'Donnell, E.	8/2/16
11430	,,	Tutty, W.	11/2/16
11494	,,	Dale, A.	11/2/16
1586	Cpl.	Wallington, A.	13/2/16
1787	Pte.	McAlister, W.	13/2/16
4638	,,	McCue, T.	8/3/16
18187	,,	Hoare, J.	24/7/16
1272	Sgt.	Lynch, J.	24/7/16
21298	Pte.	Jones, C.	24/7/16

IN THE GREAT WAR

No.		Rank and Name.	Date.
16034	Pte.	Crook, C. H.	24/7/16
4541	,,	Gladwell, A. V.	24/7/16
1724	,,	Herbert, F.	24/7/16
6297	,,	Seager, R. F.	24/7/16
14308	,,	Taylor, M.	24/7/16
22514	,,	Hook, F.	24/7/16
11898	,,	Ellis,	5/8/16
16722	,,	Hobbs, O.	14/9/16
10367	,,	Brown, G.	15/9/16
13071	,,	Richardson, J.	15/9/16
514	,,	Langton, J.	20/9/16
15875	L./Cpl.	Bartlett, A.	20/9/16
9609	Pte.	Brock, E.	17/10/16
4700	L./Cpl.	Pearce, J.	17/10/16
10228	Pte.	Walker, A.	28/3/17
14323	,,	Mollard, F.	28/3/17
11454	,,	Pountney, H.	9/4/17
6626	,,	Beard, H.	9/4/17
4508	,,	Plaister, E.	11/4/17
6702	,,	Smith, W.	2/6/17
10858	,,	Goulding, T.	2/6/17
6150	,,	Coskrey, R. A. C.	2/6/17
6052	L./Cpl.	Watts, B.	4/6/17
10003	Sgt.	Aedy, T. E.	5/6/17
32530	Pte.	Christian, M.	5/6/17
14409	,,	Meredith, A.	5/6/17
4720	,,	Taylor, J.	5/6/17
14233	,,	Galyer, J.	5/6/17
9946	,,	Carroll, J.	7/6/17
7048	,,	Pugh, W. F.	7/6/17
7018	Sgt.	Abdy, H. C.	7/6/17
10268	L./Cpl.	Sloane, E.	7/6/17
13212	Pte.	Kealing, M.	7/6/17

THE 4TH (QUEEN'S OWN) HUSSARS

No.	Rank	and Name.	Date.
14572	Pte.	Wood, W.	7/6/17
4275	,,	Fazakerley, A.	9/6/17
110	,,	Fitzsimons, W.	18/6/17
8569	,,	Freeman, C.	18/6/17
8579	,,	Duke, W. G.	18/6/17
9942	,,	Walshe, M.	18/6/17
10019	,,	Grant, R.	18/6/17
10067	,,	Griffin, C.	20/6/17
10083	,,	Eaglestone, C. W.	21/6/17
24644	,,	Ringrose, H.	26/6/17
10077	,,	Hampton, A. H.	7/7/17
24097	,,	Sida, W. H.	7/7/17
32500	,,	Rookes, P.	7/7/17
16155	,,	Bailey, W.	27/9/17
6045	,,	Butler, R.	27/9/17
7547	,,	Murphy, P.	27/9/17
6326	,,	Roberts, C.	27/9/17
4411	,,	Clark, F.	28/9/17
13167	,,	Forward, A. S.	28/9/17
10636	,,	Bending, W. H.	28/9/17
10241	Cpl.	Thrower, W.	6/10/17
10235	Pte.	Harper, G.	6/10/17
7814	,,	Sargent, W. H.	6/10/17
32574	,,	Bellington, W.	6/10/17
10011	,,	Matthews, H.	7/10/17
24916	,,	Hughes, E.	7/10/17
10096	,,	Rohan, J.	9/10/17
18218	,,	Vinton, P. H.	9/10/17
32531	,,	Gardiner, F.	27/11/17
14259	L./Cpl.	Noble, J.	27/11/17
11255	Pte.	Irwin, E. C.	28/11/17
10011	,,	Matthews, H. E.	28/11/17
9036	,,	King, J.	28/11/17

IN THE GREAT WAR

No.	Rank and Name.	Date.
45190	Pte. Elliott, W.	28/11/17
2868	,, Berry, E.	28/11/17
18042	,, Blackhall, N. E.	28/11/17
9773	L./Cpl. Walshe, J.	28/11/17
546	,, Townuroe, B. L.	28/11/17
11267	,, Emmings, G.	29/11/17
14329	Pte. Flowers, A.	29/11/17
18299	,, Dawkins, S.	29/11/17
266288	,, Hogwood, A.	29/11/17
45200	,, Paterson, P. H.	29/11/17
1532	,, Carter, T. C.	29/11/17
10388	,, Halliday, J.	29/11/17
15886	,, Sims, E. W.	29/11/17
45198	L./Cpl. Burke, J.	29/11/17
18046	,, Rowley, B.	29/11/17
255966	Pte. Smith, H.	29/11/17
24537	,, Smith, J.	3/1/18
45178	,, Jelliffe, F.	14/1/18
10066	,, Peale, S. E.	14/1/18
11614	L./Cpl. Tuppin, G.	16/1/18
412	Sgt. Baker, F.	22/1/18
10387	Pte. Watson, T.	22/1/18
32509	,, Rice, F.	22/1/18
13414	,, Walker, W.	22/1/18
1983	S.S.M. Browne, J.	22/3/18
9774	Sgt. Kavanagh, M.	22/3/18
280845	Pte. Frost, A.	22/3/18
1272	Sgt. Lynch, J.	23/3/18
18770	L./Cpl. Brooks, W.	23/3/18
45217	Pte. White, G. A.	23/3/18
2725	,, Wood, H.	23/3/18
4550	,, Marshall, W. G.	23/3/18
8813	,, Oliver, J.	23/3/18

THE 4TH (QUEEN'S OWN) HUSSARS

No.	Rank	and Name.	Date.
30418	Pte.	Shergold, J. F.	23/8/18
18358	,,	Parkinson, A. F.	23/8/18
8763	,,	Morphy, W. E.	23/8/18
174	,,	Hammond, H. W.	23/8/18
7139	,,	Bonner, F.	23/8/18
14421	,,	Pugh, A. R. E.	23/8/18
3733	Sgt.	Lawler, G. H.	23/8/18
7028	L./Cpl.	Ingle, G.	23/8/18
18203	,,	Walsh, J.	23/8/18
18324	Pte.	Warne, W.	23/8/18
45208	,,	Simmonds, C.	23/8/18
45295	,,	Taylor, H.	23/8/18
8984	,,	Tidswell, J.	23/8/18
8771	,,	Boddington, F.	23/8/18
9978	,,	Dillon, A.	23/8/18
45267	,,	Martin, A. E.	23/8/18
45284	,,	Flaherty, J.	23/8/18
10261	,,	Everitt, G. W.	23/8/18
10377	,,	Dobson, R.	23/8/18
8577	,,	Taylor, A.	23/8/18
45202	,,	Price, A. E.	23/8/18
21103	,,	Bowdon, F.	23/8/18
13020	,,	Kavanagh, T.	23/8/18
320514	Tptr.	Parsons, W. J.	23/8/18
9280	Pte.	Delaney, L.	24/8/18
11441	Cpl.	Wood, A. V.	24/8/18
9933	Pte.	Kelly, H.	24/8/18
45468	,,	Sully, F.	25/8/18
14223	Cpl.	Burgiss, W.	25/8/18
45294	,,	Hanrahan, H.	25/8/18
8788	Pte.	Hayes, W.	25/8/18
11949	,,	Silk, W.	25/8/18
15998	,,	Baldwin, W. G.	25/8/18

IN THE GREAT WAR

No.	Rank	Name	Date
10074	Cpl.	Clarke, R.	26/3/18
45225	,,	Dickens, W.	26/3/18
14181	L./Cpl.	Leigh, G.	26/3/18
9036	Pte.	King, J.	26/3/18
11117	Tptr.	Anderson, E.	26/3/18
45269	Pte.	McGregor, W.	26/3/18
6729	,,	Wilson, H. E.	26/3/18
320680	,,	Cullett, J.	26/3/18
1246	,,	Waters, J.	26/3/18
45292	,,	Bishop, C.	26/3/18
7824	,,	Groome, F. B.	26/3/18
45234	,,	Ovenden, C.	26/3/18
45203	S./Sgt.	Lyons, J.	26/3/18
45287	Pte.	O'Toole, J.	26/3/18
45210	,,	Bennett, J.	26/3/18
7856	S./Cpl.	Lane, V.	30/3/18
6056	Cpl.	Lowe, R.	30/3/18
9773	L./Cpl.	Walshe, J.	30/3/18
13947	,,	Dwyer, J.	30/3/18
9787	Pte.	Mills, W. J.	30/3/18
9944	,,	Street, G.	30/3/18
12972	,,	Howard, P.	30/3/18
10361	L./Cpl.	Stowell, G.	30/3/18
45276	S.Q.M.S.	Horan, M.	31/3/18
45291	Sgt.	Bullen, F. J.	31/3/18
2297	Cpl.	Stewart, G. H.	31/3/18
45278	,,	Lawlor, W.	31/3/18
1263	S./Cpl.	Quilty, M.	31/3/18
10084	L./Cpl.	Hazeltine, W.	31/3/18
642	,,	Lemon, D.	31/3/18
16621	,,	Denny, H. E.	31/3/18
15875	,,	Bartlett, L.	31/3/18
45280	,,	Short, R.	31/3/18

THE 4TH (QUEEN'S OWN) HUSSARS

No.	Rank and Name.	Date.
10991	L./Cpl. Gregory, J.	31/3/18
10361	,, Stowell, G.	31/3/18
1583	,, Groom, L.	31/3/18
10624	,, Crawford, J.	31/3/18
1291	S./Sgt. Devlin, M.	31/3/18
9851	Pte. Davidson, R.	31/3/18
5705	,, Coulby, H.	31/3/18
9909	,, Manning, R.	31/3/18
45253	,, McKeover, J.	31/3/18
4544	,, Smy, H.	31/3/18
25055	,, Mattine, W.	31/3/18
5132	,, Stayle, J.	31/3/18
7828	,, Gibson, F.	31/3/18
32505	,, Hamilton, S.	31/3/18
8112	L./Cpl. Nicholas, W.	31/3/18
6151	Pte. Cooke, A. W. L.	31/3/18
11616	,, Dudley, W.	31/3/18
22589	,, Spencer, W.	31/3/18
10248	,, Mitchell, J. W.	31/3/18
22514	,, Hook, F.	31/3/18
18663	,, Mathers, C.	31/3/18
8375	,, Thursby, W.	31/3/18
16130	,, Riley, M.	31/3/18
45215	L./Cpl. Munns, T.	31/3/18
14256	Pte. Moore, N. H.	31/3/18
11256	,, Abwynne, W.	31/3/18
1982	,, Cairns, A.	5/4/18
115	,, Doran, J.	9/4/18
11631	,, Bannister, M.	15/4/18
31899	,, Williams, J. D.	23/4/18
8397	Cpl. Latimer, A.	1/8/18
4476	S./Sgt. Shelton, H. E.	9/8/18
45171	Cpl. Gilchrist, G.	9/8/18

IN THE GREAT WAR

No.	Rank and Name.	Date.
45252	Pte. Healey, E.	9/8/18
45195	,, Wood, E. J.	9/8/18
14376	,, Parslon, M.	9/8/18
24644	,, Ringrose, H.	9/8/18
1237	,, Donohoe, L.	9/8/18
31850	,, O'Rourke, T.	9/8/18
6321	Tptr. Hewitt, J.	9/8/18
5565	Pte. Hipperson, T. A.	9/8/18
14867	,, Wilmot, P.	9/8/18
13038	,, Reid, P.	9/8/18
13463	,, Stanley, H.	9/8/18
45210	,, Bennett, J.	9/8/18
265581	,, Dockrell, J.	9/8/18
10228	,, Walker, A.	9/8/18
10056	Pte. Hillier, R. E.	10/8/18
22514	,, Hook, F.	10/8/18
24186	,, Warrenn, F.	10/8/18
2802	S.S.-Cpl. Perry, G.	10/8/18
11283	L./Cpl. Trappe, T.	10/8/18
6089	Pte. Tull, W. J.	10/8/18
45179	,, Marsh, G.	10/8/18
5387	,, Purcell, J. M.	10/8/18
9381	,, Mitchell, L.	10/8/18
23868	,, Oakley, C.	10/8/18
3273	Tptr. Mabbett, H. M.	10/8/18
11621	Pte. Commins, M.	10/8/18
35425	,, Blundell, J.	10/8/18
320753	,, Forrest, J.	10/8/18
9773	Cpl. Walshe, J.	24/8/18
13165	Pte. Clarke, A.	24/8/18
9402	L./Cpl. Reenan, R.	24/8/18
5494	Pte. Doggett, R. J.	24/8/18
42109	L./Cpl. Rubenstien, L.	6/10/18

THE 4TH (QUEEN'S OWN) HUSSARS IN THE GREAT WAR

No.	Rank and Name.	Date.
16030	Pte. Hall, H.	19/10/18
35398	,, Gilbert, C. C.	19/10/18
33550	,, King, C. E.	10/11/18